Nobody's Best Friend

by
Lorraine Houston

Thank you for caring!

Lorraine Houston

MCE Press
Chester, NJ

Nobody's Best Friend
by Lorraine Houston

ACKNOWLEDGMENTS

I will be forever grateful to the Toronto Humane Society for giving me the opportunity to learn and work alongside some of the country's finest animal caregivers. Although it is difficult to name all the folks who made such a difference, a special mention goes to my co-workers Marina, Irene, Nadine, Diane, Deb, and to shelter managers Sandra and Valerie for allowing me the leeway and support needed to help the dogs. Special thanks to veterinarians Dr. Peter Copeland and Dr. John Allen for always being patient and understanding when I would bring a dog to them for advice and treatment.

Sondra B. Holgate brought me into the world of dog obedience and became my second mother. She introduced me to so many wonderful people and dogs. Maggie and Ada, two of those special people, were such pleasures to work with.

Ian Dunbar has to be congratulated for changing the dog training industry with his candid, humorous ways. He is responsible for so many owners treating their dogs with kindness and respect.

Bonnie Hamilton was one of my first "doggy" friends in New Jersey. I wish to thank her for reading a chapter a week and for encouraging me along.

To Karen for listening endlessly to my tales of woe and for being my sounding board when I think that I just can't continue in this field.

To Ian, my husband, I can only say thank you for being you.

Heather Walters, my publisher, I thank you for taking this book and believing in it, and for all the time and effort you have put forth to make it better.

Last, but never least, are all the dogs that live in my heart and will be cherished there always.

DEDICATION

To all the dogs who wait in shelters everywhere hoping for the love they so deserve. And to those unfortunate creatures who are neglected, tied to chains, painfully abused and/or ill-treated.

CONTENTS

Introduction

This book is written for people who love dogs and want to share the experiences of a young woman (at the time) who worked at one of the largest animal shelters for almost 13 years, devoting both heart and soul. I feel a need to share with readers the most rewarding work I have ever had the pleasure of doing. Shelter work is not for all, and I have been asked many times over the years, "do you become hardened by this work?" My answer has always been the same: "If I have become hardened, I shouldn't be here".

If anything, I believe I have become more passionate. The more I learned about dogs, the more I wanted to do better by them. I will take you through the years of "foster" dogs that shared our home, made me wiser, humbled me, and even some that broke my heart.

In my fantasy world, every dog has a home where they are cared for, loved, respected and brought to the fullest of the human/canine relationship. In the real world, there are dogs in every shelter, in every city, every day of every week, due to lack of human commitment. Oh, there are reasons and excuses: moving, allergies, time constraints, lack of housetraining, size, noise, and the list goes on. Anyone who has worked in the field has heard them all.

In my experience, over 80% of surrendered dogs would still be in their original homes, if only humans could learn the art of communication with canines. I will share some of my ideas and successes with you, in the hope they might help some animals avoid rejection. Please understand I am not here to pass judgment. In some cases rehoming a dog is the only avenue open. But all too often no effort has been made on the part of the owner to accommodate the family dog - or simply put, dogs become homeless because they have become inconvenient.

Let me start by explaining what a "foster" home is. The word itself is pretty self-explanatory. The reasons for fostering a dog vary. An immature puppy, a convalescing dog, overcrowding, temperament evaluation - all are reasons I may have had an extra body in my car the night I drove home.

When a dog arrived at our shelter it was typically held for seven days. The hope was that the owners would come in and claim the dog during this "stray time". After the seven day holding period, the dog legally belonged to the shelter. A determination was then made whether to attempt an adoption, or, for health or temperament reasons, euthanize the animal.

Our shelter began the fostering program for dogs which the shelter manager or veterinarian believed would do better in a home environment. Some dogs I fostered for medical reasons, basically providing a place to recuperate after surgery. Like humans, most dogs will recover better in a relatively peaceful environment. For others, fostering was a way for me to evaluate the dog's temperament in a more natural home setting. Typically these were dogs I was already working with at the shelter, so I already had a good idea of what to expect.

On very rare occasions, we would temporarily take dogs into our home because the shelter had too many animals and not enough cages available. Thankfully, this happened infrequently and these foster stays did not last long.

When our foster missions were accomplished, the dogs returned to the shelter for adoption. For a brief period, I also conducted private adoptions under a program I called Canine Connections.

Successful, long-term placement is always the goal, but I'll never fully get used to seeing one of my foster friends drive away - even though I know it's the best thing for them. Sometimes, by conscious choice or circumstance, one of my foster companions makes the transition from temporary houseguest to permanent resident. Today, each of the four dogs in my house is a shelter dog turned soulmate. Some of their stories, as well as those of other dogs I've fostered, are in the pages that follow.

When I started my career in the early 1980's, we did not have an official foster care program. It wasn't until the latter part of the decade that the program was recognized. This one program has saved the lives of thousands of animals in just one shelter. I am proud that I was able to participate.

A PRAYER FOR DOGS

Good master, bless each dog that no one owns,
That has no flowerbed to bury bones,
No loving hand to scratch his ears,
No gate to guard and never quite enough to eat.
Ye saints, guard well each cringing pup, That slinks with tail
turned down instead of up.
All other dogs, beloved, gay and free,
Are blessed enough-they need not trouble thee.

- Author Unknown

MY

FOSTER

FRIENDS

BINGO

I had been working at the animal shelter for eight months. Back then, a dog that came down with kennel cough was not in a good situation. This menacing virus would spread quickly throughout the kennels and infect the other dogs. At that point in time there was no room in which to isolate the "coughers".

I had already acquired a habit of becoming "attached" to some of the dogs. My latest charge was a Basenji mix, approximately 2 years old, who had been found by an animal control officer rummaging through garbage behind a downtown Toronto mall. I remember it like it was yesterday. Joan (who was in charge of lost and found dogs) came to my co-worker Susan and myself to say she had a very scared, dear dog in and asked if we could work with him.

I really don't recall how his very smelly anal gland fluid ended up all over Susan, but this accident just highlighted his fright. "What a terrified, pathetic soul; he needs me," I thought as I bundled him into my chest. Into our cupboard of an office I took him, to get away from all the noise and confusion of the kennel. I must have sat with him on my knees for a good half-hour, stroking him gently, and speaking words that had no meaning. He made no move to jump away or to befriend me. My shift was coming to an end, so he had to go back to the kennel. "I'm sorry to put you back, fella," I murmured as I tried to arrange the blanket around him in a snugly fashion.

The next day I could not wait to get to work to see how he had survived the night. "Maybe he's not even there," I worried. "Surely he belongs to someone". I figured he must have been claimed; no one could lose such a treasure. As you have probably already guessed, he was still there, practically in the same position I had left him the evening before. Wait, was that was a spark of recognition? Or was I was only fooling myself? I spoke softly to him (which, if you knew me, is hard to believe. I am surely half-deaf after working with all the barking for so long) and opened his cage. I decided to take him out so he could relieve himself, and that he did!!

Over the next few days our relationship strengthened and grew, and soon (if no one came for him) he would be available for adoption. We used to let him stay in the office with us all day while we carried on with our daily routine of interviewing potential homes and keeping all the adoption animals clean and tidy. It was becoming crystal clear that I belonged to him and vice-versa. My new friend would monitor every move I made with great interest. Dare I leave the office to conduct an interview? Not without help. Each night as I tucked him into his cage I went home and could not stop thinking about this dog. I felt guilty for misleading him. I was sending him a strong message that we were a team.

As strange as this story sounds, it did not enter my mind to adopt "Bingo" as he was now being called. I had fallen head over heels with many dogs in the past eight months, and all had been successfully placed. At the time, my husband and I were renting a flat in a renovated old home that had been transformed into a six-plex, not far from where I worked. We also shared our lives with three cats. The landlord had two yorkies and no mention was ever made about a pet policy.

One night I was working late and I thought I heard Bingo - yes, I was right - and he was sitting on his favorite office chair coughing. Well, that was that! I couldn't put him back with the other dogs, foster care hadn't been "invented" then, and my soulmate was certainly not going to be euthanized!!! As I reached for the telephone a feeling of unknown excitement was in my bones. As soon as my husband Ian answered, I was talking a mile a minute racing out the story about the unknown fate of my trusted friend. Almost before I could hang up the phone and explain to my co-worker what was happening, my husband had arrived.

Bingo remained curled up on his chair and decided this man was not worth bothering with. I stood up and proudly motioned to the sleepy animal. "This is him," I boasted. Ian looked at the little tan figure with ears as big as deer, a face almost "dingolike" and the sharp attentive eyes. The eyes told a story of pain, truth, wisdom, eagerness, and inquiry all in one brief glance. "Do we have to sign any papers?" he asked. I cried and laughed all at once, as I moved around the room gathering my belongings, Bingo following my every step.

As we drove home our conversation was of walks in the park, obedience classes, dog food, supplies, and anything and everything that had to do with sharing your life with a canine. Unfortunately, as we pulled into the driveway and emerged with our prize, the landlord appeared. He made it more than clear that not only did he not share our enthusiasm but was quite annoyed. I boldly questioned his two little dogs, and was told there is a difference between renting and owning a property and more or less to put it in my ear. So, we were off to a dandy start. To his credit, our landlord did say Bingo could stay - as long as there was no trouble.

Trouble, and more than enough of it, is what we proceeded to have. It started with the barking complaints from the neighbours on either side. So we hired a dogsitter the next time we had an evening engagement. Then came the barking complaint from the lower neighbour who worked nights and was trying to sleep during the day. And then there was the time Ian arrived home from work and called to tell me that he was looking at what appeared to be a couch frame with several springs jutting upwards. The room was full of stuffing from floor to ceiling, with Bingo in the center of the action. He had apparently decided to have a helping of "couch du jour" while we were both at work.

There was also the case of the missing coffee break cookies. This anecdote did not cause us any complaints; it was just a mystery. I was sure I had purchased them, but maybe didn't actually put them in my cart... About a week later I noticed a crumb collection on the bed. It wasn't until the dead of night that we heard some muffled crunching sounds. Upon further investigation, we found Bingo having a midnight snack in the closet. The dear soul had carried the cookies to his hideout, where he would have a cookie or two when he fancied. There was over half a box left when all had been discovered.

Another evening, we had to attend a wedding so we again hired a dogsitter, but when we returned there was a note on the door that read: "Either you go or the dog goes!" Strange, we thought. Even stranger was the fact that when we went upstairs to our little apartment, there was no dogsitter. There was another note that read: "Left early had to go home". The young man who was dogsitting was a responsible individual, so we hoped there was no emergency. There were a couple of "poops"; nothing had been chewed, but Bingo had obviously been barking.

We spoke to the landlord the next day, but he was firm about his note. He had too many unhappy tenants, which we could appreciate. Had I known then what I know now about training dogs, I could have prevented this whole big mess. Instead, we made the decision to look for another place to live.

Before I met Ian, I had been working three jobs. Call me crazy, but it just happened that I did and I was able to handle them so I kept them all. Two of them were part-time waitress jobs and one was an office job. As you can imagine, I was busy. I was so busy I had no time to spend my hard-earned money. I just stashed it away in the bank. By no means was it a fortune, but between that and Ian's savings we had just enough for a small down payment on a house within budget! So we bought a house because of Bingo. To this day, we thank him. It was the best investment we ever made, and we probably wouldn't have done it had we not been forced to find a solution to our little "Doggy" problem.

After we moved into our new house, Bingo still continued to be destructive when left alone. We had to take him to the vet's office for a checkup, and while he was being examined, we mentioned the problem about his chewing. The vet rummaged through some paperwork and came up with an article regarding crate training. We were apprehensive about trying this method; sensing our doubt, our vet tried to expand on the article. "Dogs by nature are denning creatures," he said. "The crate provides security rather like a cave or den. If introduced properly, the dog will enjoy and seek out his 'castle'. And to be quite honest, how much more damage can you afford?"

We agreed it all made good sense, and I was now very interested in the article I held in my hand. That one little article got me started. I began to read everything I could get my hands on that had to do with dogs. Ian constructed a crate for Bingo from the instructions we had been given. We introduced him slowly and positively to his new home-within-our-home. I put a blanket and some chewies in, and he seemed to be quite cozy.

Bingo has always been nervous of thunderstorms. One evening we had a dandy storm brewing. I couldn't find Bingo anywhere, and even when I called him to me, my shadow did not appear. I ran downstairs to see if he had accidentally been closed off in the recreation room. As I walked by his crate there he was, all curled up where the storm couldn't find him. As time passed he became more familiar with daily routines and more confident that we really were coming home every time we went out. We started leaving him out of the crate for short periods of time. Often we would return and find him in his den anyway, and most important, the destructive behaviour ended.

The following years were an adventure for all of us. Bingo saw me through the birth of our first son, Ben. He would get up with me every night and help me nurse the baby. I had one of those intercom boxes and when I was really tired, I would get mixed up and think it was the radio and try to "turn off" the baby. Bingo would jump on the bed and stick his wet nose right in my ear until I got up. He was more help than any new mother could have asked for.

At the time of this writing Bingo is approximately 14 years old. His eyes have clouded over and his hearing is not quite what it used to be, although I'm sure he could still hear a crying baby. He has been with us 12 years now, and he sleeps most of the day, but still enjoys his outings. His blonde coat has been replaced by white, and he remains the apple of his adoptive mother's eye.

Ages ago a heartfelt prayer
Arose from a man in deep despair
"Oh God" he pleaded, "hear my cry
A weak and selfish sinner am I.
Deserted alike by friend and foe
No way to turn, no place to go.
Though I deserve such misery
Oh God, restore some hope to me".

The Father heard, "His need is great
For such poor mortals I'll create
A loyal friend, who'll stay close by
To love, to share, who'll ask no more
Than just to worship and adore,
A friend who'll never criticize,
Will never question or advise,
Who cannot speak or lift a hand
To help-but will just understand".
And so it came to pass, at morn
An answered prayer---A DOG WAS BORN

- Author Unknown

CHICO

How anyone could lose this ancient dog was beyond me, but there he sat in all his glory growling and lunging at the world as it went by. He was in the bottom cage, and nobody could walk by without being charged by six pounds of ferocious Chihuahua. The few teeth he had left were highly visible when he came to a shuddering halt as he met the front of the steel bars. He was a tough old bird; there was no denying that.

He quickly gained popularity among the staff, but obviously not for his congeniality. Every time we had to move him, he created havoc with his snapping and growling. One of the more seasoned staff members kindly brought in some heavy gloves (generally used for raccoons) so we could pick him up without fear of being bitten. I had to hand it to this guy; he was going nowhere fast. No lost reports had been submitted for him and it was hard to believe that someone didn't miss his presence.

I started calling him "Bubbles", but don't ask me why. I guess I just thought he looked like a bubble. He was in the room I had been assigned and it was his turn to be cleaned. I told him how handsome he was, and how nice it would be not to bite Lorraine. He really didn't have many teeth and probably not a whole lot of power either, so I smiled, more out of respect than fear. Maybe I haven't mentioned this yet, but I adore all little dogs, so I had already set my sights on this old grump. I couldn't have planned the next moment better had I tried.

I was talking to him and opening his cage slowly as he charged toward the small crack and landed right in my lap. I steadied his rump before he had time to think, stood up, and lo and behold I had one surprised Chihuahua in my arms. I think he was stunned, rather shocked, that someone cared (or dared) to hold him. As he made no effort to squirm away, I continued our embrace. I thought a quiet break was in order, so we proceeded to the kitchen to find my new friend a cozy blanket. He seemed to be assessing the situation as his bulgy eyes scanned the latest change of scenery. I had many dogs to take care of, so this little "let's get acquainted party" was soon to be over.

I had already prepared his new cage, so I tucked him up under my arm, spread his blanket out, and gently lowered him onto it. It was my turn to be shocked. Bubbles put his feet up against the bars and was asking me to please come back and play some more. I touched his tiny feet and promised, but later. Now every time I walked by his cage he perked up instead of charged. "Well now, he's coming along nicely," I thought to myself. Keeping my promise, I put a note on his cage in case anyone was looking for him, and took him to have lunch with me.

We had a dandy time. I ate, he mooched, and we connected. We only had one obstacle. He wasn't the biggest social buzz around. One friend seemed to be plenty for him, and it appeared I was it. I tried without success to introduce him to co-workers; he would have no part of it.

I was at the clinic one morning checking on a neuter operation when the receptionist asked how my latest charge was coming along. "I think he would be a fine little dog for a quiet home with a nice lady," I predicted, adding "but if he had to cope with a lot of action and small children, it would be a disaster, I'm sure." The receptionist looked at me thoughtfully, as if something were on her mind, and then proceeded to tell me about her mother who had just lost her 14-year-old terrier mix to cancer. She had asked her daughter to keep an eye open for a small apartment dog. She lived alone and the sunshine in her life had been her wee dog.

I suggested that she mention Bubbles to her mom and see what kind of reaction she got. I had asked the vet to age Bubbles and he came up with 10 years plus. It was possible her mother would not be interested in an older dog, as she had just had to deal with the loss of her other dog. She promised to mention it to her mom. It was a long shot, so I didn't get my hopes up too high. His "stray" time was almost up and still no one had reported losing this fellow.

He and I had become closer than ever, and staff used to joke about when I would sign adoption papers for the incorrigible brat. I looked in the request file for people who had left their names for small dogs and started to call a few. Unfortunately, the homes that would have been suitable were not interested in such an old dog, but reminded me to call them if I got anybody in who was younger.

I thanked them anyway, as I tried to think of some alternative ideas.

I considered taking him myself, but Ben, our first son, was only nine months old and knowing that adopting Bubbles wouldn't be realistic, dismissed it from my mind. I asked our shelter manager if he could go up for general adoption. He told me that Bubbles was not suitable because he still lunged and carried on in the cage, and he would allow no one to get near him. I knew in my heart that if he were placed properly it would be a success, and was told that if I could find a suitable home for him, I had the shelter manager's blessing to go ahead and adopt him out.

As if angels had been listening, the receptionist came over from the clinic to tell me her mother was keen on meeting Bubbles, and asked me if tomorrow afternoon would be a good time! I briefed the manager and set the wheels in motion. I made it clear that Bubbles would probably not make a good first impression on the mother. She understood this.

It is such a small world that when "Evelyn" came to the shelter the next afternoon, she looked vaguely familiar to me. "I'm certain we know each other, or have met before, but I can't for the life of me remember," I stated, smiling at the older woman. "I think I know," she said. "You are Helen's granddaughter, aren't you?" I certainly was, but how did Evelyn make the connection? "You visit your grandmother often, and not only is your gram my friend, we live only two apartments away from each other." Now it all came to me. I remembered a brief introduction made to me by my dear grandmother to Evelyn about a year ago. I had to hand it to Evelyn for having such a sharp memory.

Getting down to business, I brought Bubbles out and showed him off. Evelyn liked him right away, despite his rather antisocial outlook on life. She was confident that he would adjust and the loyalty he was showing towards me would soon transfer to her and I totally agreed. She wasn't worried, she explained, as it was only she and her bird for him to adapt to, and she admitted to being somewhat of a recluse herself. Evelyn signed the adoption contract and I accompanied her to her car and plunked Bubbles in the back seat. I had given Evelyn my home phone number in case she needed it.

I am a worrywart by nature, inherited from my grandmother, so I called Evelyn that evening. To my delight, everything was going great. The key to Bubbles' heart was through his stomach, Evelyn discovered, and within two hours he was following her around the apartment. "Another happy ending!" I proclaimed to my husband as I hung up the phone. Within a two-week period I touched base with Evelyn twice. Everybody was happy; even her little budgie liked Bubbles now.

The front desk staff paged my name to come to the lobby for a visitor late one afternoon. I immediately saw Evelyn and Bubbles waiting in the chairs. "Hey, how ya doing?" I boomed, thinking how nice it was of her to come all the way downtown to visit. Bubbles recognized my voice and wiggled over to say his hellos. "He looks great!" I complimented.

My happy face looked into Evelyn's, who was not smiling back. A deep cloud of concern was in her eyes, and her lips quivered as she spoke. "I just can't keep him, Lorraine. I am so very sorry." I didn't understand. I was confused; a thousand questions popped into my head. Maybe she was ill, maybe Bubbles was ill. "What's wrong?" were the only words that came out. "Well, I...", she stumbled. "You see, I have grandchildren who visit once in a while, and well, he is, um, he just hates them!"

Many solutions went through my mind, but if Evelyn had her mind made up, there was little I could do or say. The first thing I had to ascertain was if he had actually bitten anyone. I figured he would break his tooth off before he would break skin, but I had to ask, to comply with health and safety regulations. No, she explained, he didn't bite the children; he just chased them around and barked at them. Bubbles was sitting in my lap now, trying to get comfortable for a nap. To say the least, I was disappointed and frustrated. I scooped Bubbles into my arms and asked Evelyn if she was absolutely sure this was a final decision. Nodding her head, I asked her to sign him back in. I took him into the office with me to contemplate his situation. Too much thinking puts a burden on your brain. I came up blank every time.

Tracy, a co-worker, came into the office and was dumbfounded to hear Bubbles had been returned. "I think you should just take him home yourself, and put an end to the whole thing!" she stated. "How long do you think he honestly has? If you are lucky, maybe a couple of years; he just needs a retirement home for his golden years, and will probably sleep most of the time." "We know how much he enjoys children; do you really think it's fair?" I sarcastically questioned her. "Just keep them separated if you have to. He's so small; just pick him up!" I really had never seen Tracy so convinced before. She had been working at the shelter since the mid-seventies and had been one of many who had taught me the ropes in adoption. "Well, maybe I should just take him."

I called Ian at work and told him about this old, pathetic, soon to pass on, small, very small, dog that I was in love with and could I have him. "Use your best judgment," was his answer. I always love calling Ian at work. He can't wait to get me off the phone, and I know he'll say anything to get me to hang up. I turned to Tracy with a smile a mile wide. "I'll get the forms ready," she said, looking pretty darned pleased with herself.

The veterinarian on duty was walking by and I ran out to tell him of my latest treasure. He looked at the lump sitting in the crook of my arm and appeared doubtful. He gently tried to tell me what I already knew: "He's a very old dog dear, you realize you may not have him very long?" He tried to take a look at his teeth and was promptly told to hit the road. "He's a feisty little rascal," he chuckled. "You bring him over to the clinic later this week and I'll run some tests on him for you, just to make sure everything is in the right place." I laughed, and promised to make an appointment.

Our shift was ending and I got Bubbles ready to go to his new home. My, that sounded good. He must have known something was happening, because he kept running to the door and running back. "I'm coming, I'm coming!" Boy, was he demanding! Tracy wished us the best and was still beaming.

He was a fine little traveler, I found out as we drove home. Ian was waiting at the door, probably regretting not talking longer on the phone. He was holding Ben in his arms and looking to see who the latest addition was. I tucked Bubbles under my arm, and went up to the door waving. "I'm going to take him to the backyard," I shouted through the glass. Ian thought he would let Bingo out to meet his new roomy. So while I was in the yard, Bingo came running over to greet me and was met by this miniature Cujo canine. They sniffed each other all over and resumed toilet duties. That was easy. I picked Bubbles up and brought him into the house. "Isn't he just the cutest thing?" I asked Ian, holding him slightly forward. "Hmmm," was his reply.

No matter, I loved him. Bubbles followed my trail most of the evening. His highlight of the night was when I fed Ben and most of the dinner landed on the floor. Then came bath time, which called for a quick 40 winks on the towel. Bingo, being a kind and gentle soul, took no offense at the added company. He actually seemed curious about this dwarflike creature. Ben wasn't walking at the time, so he did not appear to be causing Bubbles any alarm.

After the routine was finished and Ben was asleep, Ian and I sat down to catch our breath. "Do we really have to call him Bubbles?" Ian asked, adding that he really didn't feel comfortable calling for Bubbles within earshot of the neighbours. I guess it must be a man thing. I really didn't care one way or the other, so I suggested he think of a name he liked. Hey, I was just happy to have him. We tried out several names, and I told Ian that most Chihuahuas are called Chico. As I said the name his ears perked up and he looked over. "I think we have our answer," Ian noted.

I explained that he was a very old dog and the vet cautioned we may not have him very long, and he was due for a check up appointment next week. Ian just smiled. "Chico" had wanted nothing to do with Ian all night, which seemed to suit them both just fine. We got ready for bed ourselves, and as I lifted Chico on to the bed I saw a strange look from the corner of my eye. "What?" I asked. "He can sleep on the bed, Bingo won't mind!" Ian gave up and got into bed. He leaned over to kiss me and got a face full of Chihuahua. "Oh Chico, stop", I said as I lifted him up and put him back near the bottom of the bed. From his noisy objections you might think we had a serious problem on our hands. If he were any other dog we would have, but this old bag of wind complained about everything.

Why, you may ask, would anyone want a cantankerous dog like that? I can only answer you this way: there was something magical between us from the second he fell into my lap that morning at work. He made me feel special, chosen, and I am, and always will be, the biggest pushover for any old, grumpy dog. It's just in my blood and I can't explain it. We just have something in common I guess, which doesn't say a whole lot about me; it's just the way it is. Maybe that's why I got along so well with my grandmother (not that she was grumpy, just set in her ways, so to speak).

If my records are straight, and the vet's estimate accurate, Chico is now 20 some-odd years old and still going strong. He has been my constant companion, a fearless protector, a bedside nurse, an alarm clock, and a shadow for (believe it or not) the last 9 years. He has tolerated our two boys, sometimes not very gracefully, as they have grown. As I write this story about him, he is curled up by the heat register at my feet, dreaming doggy dreams and snoring. Not a tooth left in his head now, his tongue hangs out the side of his face more than not, but he is still the first one to "charge" the door when the bell rings.

SCAMPIE

One of the cutest dogs I have ever seen (and I have seen too many) was this wire-haired, wispy tan and white terrier mix. A face for poster fame! He was about 15 pounds, aged at approximately two years, and of course wasn't neutered. Unfortunately, his bedside manner needed help. He sat in the back of his cage showing his pearly whites.

I had a feeling in my heart that this dog really was a nice guy, but he wasn't going to be an adoption candidate if he continued to show off his teeth. I went through the "let's be friends" routine, which took a while, and decided that the best place for him was my home and a private placement. I asked Barbara, the shelter manager, if Scampie could be a Canine Connections dog, and without hesitation I had the go-ahead. He fit in at our home immediately. He slept in the laundry basket and ate toast with my father-in-law every morning. After assessing that in normal, real-life situations he showed no signs of being a risky placement, I put an ad in the paper. I waited patiently for the right person to call, as always playing the waiting game.

After two weeks of running the ad, a really nice lady called to inquire. She had had a terrier mix for 14 years, Scooter, who had just recently passed away. She lived alone in a large home with a fenced yard, and was lost without a dog. We talked for a long time, or shall I say I listened, as she reminisced about her other dog. I had an uneasy feeling that maybe she wanted Scooter back, which was an impossibility.

I have interviewed enough people to know that everyone's grieving time is different. I have known some that have waited years to adopt another dog, and I have met people who come down to the shelter the same day. Grieving time is different for all of us, and should not be judged. It is also very difficult not to compare the new arrival with our familiar cherished friend; after all we are only human. Many people feel that acquiring another dog "too soon" after the death of their previous dog is disrespectful. There must be a mourning and healing period, but the memories should never be forgotten. Many areas now offer pet loss counseling and if you are have trouble coping with the death of a beloved companion, it would be something to consider.

I continued my conversation with "Jean" regarding Scampie and I described him to her. She said she would be interested in meeting him so we set up an appointment for the following day. She gave me the grand tour of her house. Scampie politely followed at my heels, and then lay by our feet while we had tea and looked at photos of Scooter. Jean had made several efforts to befriend Scampie, all which had been either ignored or rebuffed. "He appears to be quite attached," she said, looking at the two of us. I explained that this happens often with shelter dogs, perhaps because I had showed him continued kindness. It didn't help matters that Scampie's eyes never left my face and had I tried I couldn't have asked for better "eye contact" attention. However, he needed a home, and as far as I was concerned this was it. We chatted some more and during our second cup of tea, Jean announced she would like to sign adoption papers for Scampie.

Here comes the bittersweet part of this business! I drove home without Scampie. He stood looking out the window and I pretended not to see him, as I wiped my tear-filled eyes. Jean called me three days later to tell me Scampie was still looking out the window. She didn't appear to be too concerned because he took time out to eat. I would have died had she said, "Well, dear, this just isn't working out, you better come back and collect him". Fortunately, Jean had enough faith to wait for him to adjust and called me back two days later to tell me he had made the transition. He was following her around now, and slept by her side - in the bed, of course.

TO A POUND DOG

Big sad eyed dog
In kennel number four.
It's been a week now
Since your master left you there...
Seven long and lonely days.
You see...he had to leave town,
(That's what he said).
But, this you could not know
And so you watch and wait,
In silent dignity
You wait, and watch
With eyes that break my heart.

Proud head is slightly lower
As hope fades slowly.
Hour by endless hour.
Oh, would that I could stay
And comfort you.
Explain to worried eyes
You had not failed.
The fault not yours
(For so you think).
No. Not yours.
You see...it's just
he had to leave town,
(That's what he said).

- Nancy Mason

LACEY

We had just finished some renovation work to our home in the fall of 1990, adding a good deal more space for our growing family. (My thinking was that it gave me more room for my foster dogs too!) When I returned home from work one evening and let the dogs out into the backyard, something was different, but I couldn't figure out what. After I let them back in, I walked out onto the deck and looked all around. That's when it hit me - all the patio furniture was gone: table, chairs and umbrella!! I checked the yard thinking Ian had moved them for some reason, but found nothing. I went to the shed. Ian's bike was gone, and so were the hedge trimmers we had bought him for Father's Day! It finally sunk into my head that we had been robbed!

We filed the report with the police officer who came over, who told us that it was possible that the inside of our house may be the next target. He joked that if Chico were about 70 pounds bigger we wouldn't need to worry about being vandalized again. After the officer left, we were feeling vulnerable for the first time in our own home. We had been living in this house for eight years and had never had anything like this happen before. Ian, trying to lighten up the situation, joked about fostering a German shepherd, or somebody similar. I do not condone the use of dogs strictly as guard animals or watch dogs, and I felt guilty even considering the motive, but our house WAS a bit bigger now.

I told the robbery story to some co-workers the next day and was offered the same solution. Knowing full well whomever I fostered would become permanent, I made the rounds of the dogs that were still in stray time and the ones in all the other areas. I always knew which dogs were going to be available for fostering and I worked with the adoption dogs, so I popped into the diarrhea/vomiting room, making sure not to touch anyone and to wipe my boots when I left.

There stood a skinny, older looking German Shepherd mix. I went over to read the receipts. Stray female shepherd, approximately nine years old, 78 pounds, Black and Gray. I read further to find out why she was in this room. "Not eating well" and "vomiting," the chart read. The tests that had been done had all come back negative. Maybe she needed a bit of R&R (and a nice home!). I went to the phone in the office to call Ian to see if he was bluffing or whether he was open to the idea of another dog of our own. Heaven knew he was pretty seasoned by now with all the foster dogs that had come and gone. When you live with someone for many years you know what he or she is all about, and just as I had figured, Ian was interested - if I thought there was a dog at the shelter that would be suitable. I told him about the older female shepherd, and about some of the other dogs up for adoption.

Ian has always let me be the "dog" person of the family and left it up to my good judgment, but did throw in that he had always liked huskies and was a little nervous of Dobermans. Well, that sounded to me like a green light to chose a dog! It was all happening so fast and I felt just like the clients that came in to adopt, a flood of emotions were racing through me. I spoke to Mary, the assistant shelter manager, about my situation, and she suggested if I were interested in the old shepherd girl to book her out as a foster for "Stress Relief" to see if she might do better outside the shelter environment.

> **I have always felt sorry for the housebroken dogs (in the kennel) holding, waiting, holding some more, not wanting to mess their cage area.**
>
> **We humans take so much for granted!**

I couldn't wait to tell the adoption department what was going on. They were all excited for me and suggested I bring the dog into the office. I asked the vet if there was any problem in bringing her in (I like to check, in case the medical staff want to do tests or if they think the dog could be carrying anything contagious). He went in with me and read the file and said there was nothing he could see that would prevent her from coming out for a visit, and she would not spread anything. I took a leash with me into the room, which always makes me feel bad, as I pass the cages with so many faces wanting to be chosen. I opened her cage and looped the leash over her neck, and she came alive!

She jumped up at me and made a very strange primal yodeling

sound from the bottom of her toes. I decided to take her to the toilet area out back before I took her to the office, leaving everyone to wonder where I had gone. I put a note on her cage that read "OUT WITH LORRAINE". Off we went for a quickie and she had to go badly. (I always felt sorry for the housebroken dogs holding, waiting, holding some more, not wanting to mess their cage area. We humans take so much for granted!) I walked her around some more, she pulled a little, and I noticed her hind end looked weak and her back legs shook slightly while she sniffed the grass.

We finally arrived at the office to "show off" and there was nobody waiting. Oh well, I figured it would be a good time to do some serious bonding and getting to know each other. Her gray muzzle nudged my arm, sending my cup of tea flying. I started to look for some paper towels when one of the gals came back into the office. "She's a beauty," said Donna. If anyone could make the dogs "laugh", it was Donna. She would sing, dance or make funny faces just to get the dogs to wag their tails, or start a game. I hadn't thought of a name, so I asked Donna what she thought I should call her. We batted around a few names. I can't remember who said it first, but we agreed she would be called Lacey.

She was noble, refined and very dignified looking. Her head was primarily black and her body looked as if someone had taken black and gray hairs, put them in a bowl, stirred them all up, and then spread them on her body. Her toenails hadn't been cut for too long, and she had splayed or "flat" feet. Eileen (a German Shepherd fancier and a toenail fanatic) came into the office next. I had her two favorites on the end of my leash: her chosen breed; and a set of nails that needed trimming. She set to work for me as I held Lacey's head in my lap, and all went well.

I called Ian before I left to tell him I was going to come by his office to show him the newest Houston family member. Lacey was an excellent traveler. She sat in the passenger seat like the Queen of Sheba. At the red lights she would look over at the next car as if to say, "Look at me, see who I am!" I really got the feeling she thought herself quite clever. I drove to Ian's work and waited for someone to go in so I could ask them to send Ian out. A few minutes later, when he surfaced, he looked at Lacey and took her big head into his hands, stroking under her chin. She started to make that primal sound again. We both laughed and I knew he liked her and she him. We hoped the rest of the introductions would go as smoothly. One down, seven to go! I told Ian I didn't want the kids in the car and I would proceed home with Lacey if he would pick the boys up.

I put Lacey in the backyard and waited while she attended to her business. Bingo and Chico had seen enough "freeloaders" come and go so I wasn't really all that worried about their reaction. I just prayed that she would be decent to them. When I finalize adoptions to families that have an established dog at home I recommend they make their introductions on neutral territory to avoid conflict. Ideally, I ask them to bring their dog down to the shelter BEFORE signing adoption papers, to be certain of their match. Taking none of my own advice, I held the leash, while opening the door for Bingo and Chico to come into the yard. They both made little effort to acknowledge her, as they had to relieve themselves first. I watched Lacey's body language closely, not wanting to put tension on the leash for fear she might react unfavorably. Her hackles were normal, ears forward and tail was down and swinging. Good stuff!

Chico approached as he always does. "I'm the supervisor here, and who the hell are you?" Funny thing about Chico, he thinks he is Mr. Big Show, but when push comes to shove, one look from

Bingo and Chico becomes assistant supervisor very quickly. Bingo began with the usual ritual of smelling Lacey's rear end which she really didn't appreciate, but tolerated. A few more good sniffs and that was it.

I kept Lacey on the leash as we went into the house in case she took chase on one of the cats. I was hoping she would meet Bob first. He is the best "dog cat", as he refuses to run and give dogs what they want so they can chase him. I have seen the funniest antics from foster dogs as they try to start a game of chase with Bob, but he outsmarts them all. He reminds me of Garfield the cartoon cat, who has the opinion that dogs are slobbering boobs with not too much upstairs. Bob is very kind and could scratch, but his hiss and "Don't mess with me" look always get the point across. My fears were put to rest that evening with the cats. Lacey all but ignored them.

I gave Lacey a small piece of cheese just to make sure she wouldn't take half my fingers with it, because the kids would soon be home and I planned to have them offer her some. I took her outside for the meeting, giving her the option of a bit more space. When the kids got out of the car, her tail started to swing again as she moved towards them. Ian had briefed them on the ride home, and had our younger son, Stewart, tucked under his arm. I reached over and placed a tidbit of cheese in Ben's hand and gave him the okay to offer it to Lacey. She took it gracefully, and sat straight as an arrow for another piece. I gave Ben another and this time she took it and licked his hand right up to his elbow, which made him laugh, which made her continue. So, for our first day, it was a grand success. In fact, that success lasted two and a half years.

Sadly, Lacey was diagnosed with mialopathy, a crippling disease, in May of 1993. She began to deteriorate and in late June fell over and was left somewhat paralyzed from midway down the spine. It took Ian and two other fathers to carry her home from the park one afternoon. I took her to see the vet who told me what I already knew, that soon Lacey would be totally paralyzed. She seemed to have recovered from the park incident, although I knew it was just a matter of time. Lacey was an extremely proud dog and I would not have her stripped of her dignity. We had to carry her up the stairs at bedtime, and on her face was the look of total humility.

On the evening of July 8th there came a knock to the side door where Lacey used to defend her castle and her loved ones who lived inside. As she rose, the back part of her tired body refused to cooperate and my dear Lacey fell down the stairs, tumbling, turning, and twisting as she fell. I regret not setting her free from the pain sooner. It was my own selfishness that led to that dreaded fall. She would suffer no more. The next day I took work off and stayed with her, talking to and stroking her. I could not cry because it would have upset her. She knew me better than I knew myself, we had become so close. That afternoon, our neighbor Gloria took our boys to the park, while Ian and I took Lacey to the veterinarian's office to have her put to rest, to free her body from the pain and free her soul. We both stayed with her until she had taken her final breath. And then I cried.

As we were driving home the sky was becoming gloomy and a summer storm was fast approaching. As we sat on the deck a single bolt of lightening flashed through the darkness, the sky began to brighten and the storm passed over. It was a sign from my Lacey. I know it was her way of telling me she had made the journey safely.

THE RAINBOW BRIDGE

There is a bridge connecting heaven and earth.

It is called The Rainbow Bridge because of its many colors. Just this side of the Rainbow Bridge is a land of meadows, hills and valleys, all of it covered with lush green grass.

When a beloved pet dies, the pet goes to this lovely land. There is always food and water and warm spring weather. There, the old and frail animals are young again. Those who are maimed are made whole again. They are happy and play all day with each other.

There is only one thing missing. They are not with their special person who loved them on earth. So, each day, they run and play until the day comes when one suddenly stops playing and looks up! Then, the nose twitches-the ears are up! The eyes are staring! You have been seen, and that one suddenly runs from the group. When you and your special friend meet, you take him or her in your arms and embrace. Your face is kissed again and again and again, and you look once more into the eyes of your trusting pet.

Then, together, you cross the Rainbow Bridge, never again to be separated.

- Author Unknown

SIMON

While I will remember every dog I fostered until the end of time, there are always a few that come to mind instantly whenever I am asked about my work. Simon was one of those dogs. A more complete metamorphosis has never been witnessed than that of Simon.

Due to the extremely high number of dogs in the shelter, I had permission to adopt some of the dogs out of my home through Canine Connections. The shelter was in a crisis with so many dogs, and because the numbers were so high, the chance of virus and infection was also high. Although the kennel cough room was isolated from the other dogs, it too was full. We were going to have to find foster homes for some of the dogs, or start making some hard decisions that nobody wanted to make. I chose to foster a very shy shepherd mix: a blonde body covered with greasy, oily deposits, a black muzzle and every rib poking through his slender frame. Huddled in a corner, he pressed himself into the wall.

"Would you like to come home with Lorraine?" I spoke in my most happy, excited sounding tone. No response; if anything, a look of frozen fear came into his eyes at being spoken to directly. I was given my instructions regarding his medication. He was to be kept isolated from all other dogs. The way our house was set up, this was possible; I could keep Simon (as I was going to call him) in the recreation room away from my dogs and exercise them separately. I have to explain that I have been very fortunate in that never have my own dogs contracted any illnesses from my foster dogs. I am so careful because my dogs' health and welfare has always been a priority.

When I collected Simon from the kennel cough room I had only one problem. He refused to walk, so I carried him down to my car and plunked him in the back seat. At home, I set up Simon's "guest" room and his crate. I brought him downstairs and he immediately found a place to hide - behind the crate. I wasn't going to push the issue so I left him alone to become familiar with his new surroundings. During our dinner, he didn't make even a peep. (Actually the whole time I had Simon I don't remember ever hearing him bark, whine or whimper.)

I went down later to feed him. He was in the same spot where I had left him. I spoke to him and put his food down. Half an hour later I went to down to see if he had eaten and take him out to relieve himself. He hadn't eaten much, but I figured anything was better than nothing. As the days went by, the look of frozen terror and slinky body movements began to fade away. He needed a lot of confidence building and Lord knew he needed a bath, but I did not want the trust we were building to be broken.

Approximately two weeks passed. Simon had finished his medication, and his kennel cough had cleared up nicely. When I approached Barbara about finding him a home privately, she gave me the go ahead. I made several phone calls that evening to my contacts in the dog world, giving his description and his emotional needs. He would need a home where he could continue to blossom. Now that his kennel cough was gone, I could begin a little "social" work, moving slowly and positively. As you have probably noticed, I do not set my expectations very high initially. I have seen too many dogs pushed into situations where they are clearly not comfortable.

My son Ben, who was five years old at the time, started to accompany me on my walks with Simon. It was evident right from the start that Simon enjoyed children and was at ease with them. We were not as successful, however, when it came to my husband. Simon wanted nothing to do with Ian and avoided him at all cost. I had half expected this type of reaction and we decided to ignore the behaviors that were "antisocial" and make a giant fuss when he was showing signs of being "brave". He caught on quickly and was soon at least sitting in the same room as my husband.

I put an ad in the paper to open another avenue, but got no useful response. He was getting very cozy with us but I was no closer to finding him a home than when I started. Later that week, I received a call from Jane, one of the "contacts" I had made through Canine Connections. Jane had been saving dogs and cats from local pounds before I was even thought of, and placed them in homes on her own with the help of a few other women. She was calling to tell me that one of the dogs she had placed in 1978 had passed away and the family had called her to see if she was still placing pets. Jane had not been active in the adoption placement for a couple of years, so she told the people about my efforts to place homeless dogs. She also said that, if this family took Simon, I would never have to worry about his happiness again. I waited anxiously for their inquiry call to come, and it did - the very next night.

I spoke to a Mrs. Remington who explained that the loss of their almost 14-year-old spayed female lab mix had left the family devastated, especially their daughter Lucy, who had been raised with the dog. We spoke at length about Simon and arrangements were made for a visit the following evening. They were going to come over to our house at 8:00 p.m. As I was giving her the directions, we realized that our homes were less than 10 minutes from each other. I was very excited at the prospect of Simon getting an excellent home. Simon knew there was something going on that evening, because I had to use the facilities three times in less than an hour!

At exactly 8:00 there was a knock on the door and I found myself looking at a very handsome middle-aged couple and a young woman of about 22. If Bingo had been up for adoption it would have been a done deal. He made an unusually dramatic fuss over these people as if they were all lost soulmates that had been reunited. "He's mine, his name is Bingo," I explained, while trying to appear in control. In the meantime, Simon sat stone-faced on the couch and did not even acknowledge that strangers had entered our home. I put my own dogs in the bedroom to help calm the situation.

Lucy wanted to get right down to business; she suggested we take Simon for a walk. This was a perfect idea since he dearly loved his walks. I handed the leash over to Lucy about half way up the street and then I hung back with mom and dad. I watched as Lucy handled Simon and was delighted to hear her speaking softly and encouragingly to him. He looked back a couple of times to make sure I was still part of the adventure, but Lucy was keeping his attention without stressing or spooking him. Mrs. Remington must have picked up on the fact that I was impressed. "There is something happening up there between them," she motioned. I couldn't have said it better myself. Something magical was definitely happening. I knew at that moment Simon was going to be offered a home.

We returned from our walk and sat around the coffee table talking about the future of the dog who lay by our feet. Mr. Remington who, up to this point, had been a "silent" partner, was asking about the neutering of the dog. At the first sound of his voice, Simon literally jumped to the other side of the room. It was very clear, from Simon's point of view, that this man was not part of the package. It was good that they see this behaviour before they committed.

I knew in my heart that it was only a matter of time before Simon and Mr. Remington would develop a relationship, but I was not going to force their hand. The last thing Simon needed would be to be brought back. "I like him!" Lucy's voice rang clear. I suggested they have a family meeting and I excused myself. I took the opportunity to let Simon relieve himself in the backyard; besides, I could use a breath of air.

Almost as I walked back into the living room, they told me they had come to a decision. They wanted to share their lives with Simon on one condition. I looked puzzled, I'm sure. They wanted to know if they could change his name to Jake! Because he had become accustomed to the name Simon, I recommended they call him Simon-Jake for a while, softening the Simon, and eventually dropping it. If this was the only hurdle, we were in good shape.

We had tea and discussed ways to enhance the friendship between the two "men". Simon would leave with them that night. They assured me the house was anxiously awaiting the pitter-patter of dog feet again. The adoption papers were signed and they gave me a check to cover the neutering operation, which I would schedule in the near future.

The departure was as I had envisioned, and extremely emotional for both Simon and myself. He didn't want to leave and I stood there blubbering good-byes. His "miracle" family waved as they drove away, while Simon looked out the back window.

Simon-Jake would go on to become a "CGC" dog, which stands for Canine Good Citizen. Lucy and he worked very hard to achieve this goal. They now visit nursing homes and retirement facilities on a regular basis. For all the joy I received watching Simon's transformation, I can only imagine how much more happiness he now brings to all the people he visits.

MISS PENNY

"How sick is the little Yorkie?" I asked the clinic veterinarian, Dr. MacLean. He looked thoughtfully at the ragmop who sat on the examination table. "It's hard to say until we test further," was all he could say. "Well, I'm game!" I smiled confidently up at him.

This had all come about when Miss Penny Lee had been abandoned at the main clinic. Her owners refused to come and pick her up again. She had constant diarrhea and was ruining their new broadloom. Dr. Mac had always been fond of this little

hairpiece of a dog, and was looking for someone, preferably staff, to foster her while he continued to research and test what ailed her. To date,
he was at a dead end, but had some other ideas he wanted to follow through on. I checked to make sure she had nothing contagious, and all tests had come back negative. Dr. MacLean was convinced there was something going on inside that tiny body. He told me that I would have to bring her back and forth for a bit, but hopefully we could put her back on the road to recovery, and find her a new and better home. "Please tell me I can do something with her hair!" I remarked, as I fiddled with the long strands that had not been washed or brushed. He smiled. "It's hard to see the dog in there, but you can have her groomed". So off I went with Miss Penny stuck under my arm.

My husband came home that evening and remarked about "Cousin It" coming for a visit. I told him that I had already called a groomer and had an appointment for Friday morning. I had set up the room downstairs for Miss Penny. She had a lovely basket, two quilts, and her food and water. She appeared to be a quiet little rugrat, and was very tired, probably due to her illness, whatever it was.

The next morning when I went to wake her up to let her outside, I could smell a rancid odor coming from downstairs. I walked into her room and saw diarrhea everywhere. She sat in her basket shaking; pleading eyes looked up at me. I began by opening the windows, then picked her up and took her outside, and returned to the basement to clean and disinfect the floor. It was a good thing the floor was linoleum (very easy to clean up), but the smell was pretty overpowering. I called Dr. MacLean and asked him if I should bring her with me to work, and he confirmed that indeed I should.

By the end of the week she must have felt like a pincushion, so many more tests were being done. Something abnormal did come back with one of the blood tests, but I really didn't quite understand what it was. I had to give her some pills, and they did in fact firm up her stool. I had to cancel her hair appointment due to her stay at the clinic, so I rescheduled it for the following Friday.

I would sit with her all cozy in my lap at night while we watched TV. One evening she started making strange choking, gurgling sounds and I lifted her up to see what was wrong. To my utter shock, she had gone limp and was twitching and foaming. I thought she was choking on something. I tried to look down her throat, which only made things worse. I screamed for Ian to come and help me. By then she had stopped twitching and lay lifeless in my lap. To this day I thought she had passed away.

I started rubbing her and calling her name. I was panicking, but still sat rubbing and massaging. Her eyes slowly opened and I could tell she was breathing, but I still had no idea what had just happened. After a few moments, she appeared to be somewhat better, so I called the shelter to have Dr. MacLean call me. I explained to him what had occurred and he asked me many questions. She was in my arms and was quickly becoming more coherent. We decided that she had suffered a seizure of some sort, but again, the cause was unknown. I slept with her on the couch that night, just in case we had a repeat incident.

In the morning I had to take her back in to see Dr. MacLean. It seemed just when we had solved one problem, another arose. I took her over to the clinic and put her in a cage with her blanket. She really became stressed when I had to take her, but it was the only way we were going to be able to help her. When I had lunch, I brought her with me and Dr. Mac told me I could take her home when I finished work.

Weeks went by without any problems; this stool medicine was really doing the trick. She even started to become peppy and bouncy. But some test results had come back and Dr. Mac wasn't happy about them. On instinct he called a well-known veterinary college and spoke with a specialist regarding Miss Penny's case. Just as he had thought, the results all pointed to a very rare stomach disorder. In most cases, the life span of the affected dog was very limited. The specialist, after reading Miss Penny's file, concluded that she might have only about a year left to live.

So, where did that leave us? I certainly didn't think she was suffering, not at this point anyway. She was doing great. She was eating better, her bowel movements were normal, her personality had emerged, and last but not least, her hair looked lovely!

I had to think about this long and hard. I told Ian that night about Miss Penny's diagnosis, and he stated firmly that our family just couldn't keep another animal. At that time we already had three dogs and three cats. He also reminded me that we had said the same thing about Chico not having much longer - and he was still going strong eight years later.

Disappointed with Ian's answer and not wanting to think about it for the time being, I wanted to do something that didn't take much brain power, so I started playing a computer game. Miss Penny started barking and running around, almost like someone was at the door, but none of the other dogs was joining her so I figured it was a false alarm. However, I checked anyway to make her efforts seem worthwhile. Nobody was there and I resumed my game. Again, the barking and twirling started; she was at my feet now jumping and then running out to the kitchen. "What is the problem?" I asked her, unconcerned. "Quiet please". Nothing doing, she became frantic. She must be trying to tell me

SOMETHING. Maybe she had to go to the bathroom, so I got up and she immediately ran for the kitchen, which is the opposite way from the toilet area.

I followed her, and then I realized what it was she had been trying to tell me. Before I turned on the computer I had plugged in the kettle to make tea and had totally forgotten. The kettle was bone dry and had started to smoke! I reached over to unplug it, even the cord was burning hot, but I managed to grab it. I couldn't believe it. This little angel just prevented a fire from starting. I looked down at her, and she had an expression on her face I can only describe as her saying, "Finally, you listened to me!" I picked her up and smothered her with kisses. I relayed the story to family and friends. I told Ian how Miss Penny had saved our home from near disaster; he was grateful but still didn't want to keep her.

I couldn't sleep and just didn't know what to do. Finally, a week after receiving the news from Dr. MacLean, I could not come up with a solution where everyone benefited and was happy. If I took her back to the shelter, she would not be able to go up for adoption due to such a serious medical problem. I didn't blame the shelter. I knew that most people would not be interested in adopting a dog that would most likely die or have to be put to rest within 12 months. Even if they were, would they be prepared for the cost of the medicine and other expenses? Probably not.

I became depressed and at home Ian noticed the change, and knew what it was about. I had tried to broach the subject several times that week, but Ian had dug his heels in every time. In my mind, one more tiny dog who was no trouble and had already lived with us for over eight weeks was not asking that much. In Ian's mind it meant one more dog to feed, vaccinate, clean up after, and share the couch with. We married for better or worse, and I guess this situation was bringing out the "worse" part. That night I told Ian I would return Miss Penny to the shelter the next day and let the chips fall as they may, and that it was a very strong possibility that she would have to be put to sleep. I wasn't trying to make him feel guilty, honest; I just wanted him to understand the facts.

The next morning, after another sleepless night, I gathered Miss Penny's belongings together while Ian made tea. I started to cry from a combination of exhaustion and emotion. He looked at me and remarked, "I guess one more little dog won't hurt." I hugged him tightly and knew as I have always known that he was the guy for me.

At the time of this writing (some 4 years later), Miss Penny is still with us, off her medication and living life to the fullest. It is true what they say about love, it really can heal.

JOEY

It was about 4 weeks before Christmas 1991, and I have always been a big fan of the festive season. I feel all warm and giving inside, although when it comes to dogs, I feel that way all year round. I was introduced to Joey by a co-worker who brought the dog into the office. He was a black skeleton, totally emaciated, and looked like a bag of bones with fur thrown over as an afterthought. His coat was dull, his eyes were sunken and crusted. His whippet like tail swung slowly back and forth as we spoke to him.

Joey had been found wandering the streets of Toronto and had been picked up by Animal Control. He had been aged at between six and eight years old. Had he not been brought in, I'm sure he would have frozen to death in a matter of weeks. The shelter vet's office was right next door to ours and I could hear him doing paperwork, so I walked Joey over for him to see. I had already made up my mind that if I had permission, he was coming home with me.

Dr. Campbell gave him a physical examination and ordered some tests. He said the kindest thing we could do for this dog was to put him in a home environment. Barbara also approved of the idea, so it was "homeward bound" for Joey. I can't say there is any rhyme or reason to the naming of my foster dogs. Sometimes I name them myself, other times they already have a name, and I often let my boys name them. Joey was a saint from the time he set paw in my car. Despite his physical condition, he had a zest for life. I figured he might be tired and wish to rest, but I think he was too excited. He was not showing any signs of illness, and his tests came back normal, so there was no need to isolate him while we were home and supervising. He took an immediate liking to the kids.

> **There is nothing more rewarding for a child than the unconditional love of a dog.**

Children and dogs must be watched at all times, every second of every minute. I cannot stress this enough. I hear of tragedies that happen between dogs and children, and the only question that comes to mind is "Where were the parents?". It takes not even seconds for an incident to occur. So, if there are any parents reading this book, take note. If you're taking a phone call, trying to make dinner, answering the door, stop and be sure that you have not left an accident waiting to happen. It takes only a minute to crate the dog or put him in the backyard, or scoop your little one into your arms.

There is nothing more rewarding for a child than to have the unconditional love of a dog. This I know, because I had the honour of receiving that love as a youngster. However, the child must be taught kindness and appropriate handling of a dog. Toddlers can be a dog's worst nightmare. At best, toddlers are poking, pulling, screaming, dropping, squeezing, squealing machines. And this is normal, totally and completely. But for the family dog, these unpredictable actions can cause unpredictable reactions.

> **Toddlers can be a dog's worst nightmare.**
> **At best, toddlers are poking, pulling, screaming,**
> **dropping, squeezing, squealing machines.**

I always ask people to try and put themselves in the dog's position. This little person walks like she's drunk most of the time, kisses you with sticky lips one minute and in the next breath is trying to poke "Barbie" up your keester or in your ear. Do not allow children to unintentionally abuse dogs. Teach them kindness and gentleness, and as they grow tell them that dogs have feelings too. When they are old enough to understand, ask them if they would like what was happening to them if they were a dog.

If more parents took the time to teach "Humane Education" at home I believe it could change a great deal of the world we are living in, and turn a child into an adult who has a greater respect for all living creatures. I give dogs that have survived toddlerhood more credit than my charge card. These dogs are the creme de la creme. I have met many a dog that truly, sincerely and wholeheartedly love everything about kids, but parents should always err on the side of caution. Even the kindest dogs have a breaking point. It annoys me when people say "Oh, Johnny can do anything to Max and he wouldn't bite," yet if he were to do the things that a child is permitted to do to a dog, to another child in the schoolyard, he would be suspended from school.

Do not allow children to unintentionally abuse dogs.

Teach them kindness and gentleness, and as they grow tell them that dogs have feelings too.

Getting back to Joey... Christmas was fast approaching and I invited Joey to spend it at the Houston Hotel. If I had room for another dog I would have kept Joey in a blink, but I have to keep good sense in the front lobe of my brain at all times. I could no longer foster if we kept Joey and we were already at our limit for dogs in our area. His frail, bony body was slowly filling out and his coat was a beautiful, glossy sheen of blackness now.

The shelter was closed for the Christmas holidays. We were always careful around this time of year, trying hard to screen out any of our animals going home to be surprises under the tree. We enjoyed having Joey that Christmas. There were even some gifts under the tree with his name on them.

His visit with us was coming to an all too quick end; the time had come for him to find a home of his own. I took him back to the shelter and put him in the adoption room the week between Christmas and New Year's. It is always an incredibly busy time for adoptions. It was December 27th, the first day we had re-opened and the lobby was jammed with people. I had written a story about him and put it up on his cage about how absolutely delightful he was. The day was so crazy with applications, phone calls, questions and interruptions, it was hard to think straight.

When a pleasant woman popped her head in the office to ask a "few" questions about Joey, it was difficult to give her my full attention. I did tell her that I was indeed his foster mom, and that if she were seriously interested the best thing to do would be to fill out the required forms and I would try and serve her personally. Eileen, my co-worker, called her number but was kind enough to "trade" applications with me so I could meet the lady myself.

Having answered all the basic questions, I asked them what made them chose Joey out of all the other dogs (and believe me there were many homeless dogs that year!). They said that they saw gentleness, kindness and a look of quiet calm on his face, and the fact that he was an older dog appealed to them. She joked about an old dog for an old couple. The stage was set, the match was made. It was nice he was only in the shelter for about four hours.

I wish all the dogs had the good fortune that Joey did that day. As they waved good-bye in the mad house of a lobby, I could barely make Joey out in the pet supply store with all the people and animals. That was my Christmas present of 1991. Thank You Santa.

ON ABANDONMENT

A dog sits waiting
in the hot midday sun
too faithful to leave
too frightened to run.

He's been there for days now
with nothing to do
but sit by the road
just waiting for you.

He can't understand
why you left him that day
He thought you were stopping
to take him to play.

He's sure you'll come back
and that's why he stays
How long can he suffer?
How many more days?

His legs have grown weak
his throat's parched and dry
He's sick now from hunger
he falls with a sigh.

He lays down his head
and closes his eyes
I wish you could see
how a waiting & faithful dog dies.

- Kathie Flood
(reprinted from the Animal's Voice Magazine)

ADA

Ada was a beagle terrier mix, a very nervous, flitty and flighty dog, who came to the shelter as a stray. We guessed that she was about two years old. The shelter was in another crisis situation, with too many dogs and not enough space to hold them all. There was no room at the inn.

Ada was not an easy dog to work with because every sound, every movement sent her into a spinning frenzy. She would approach no one, but while we cleaned her cage, her first reaction was to try and fly past. If escape was not possible, she would go completely limp, roll over and expose her underside. I understand that a cornered dog is a high risk bite situation, and it is NOT recommended to push the issue. The only reason I came upon her submissive reaction is because she offered it very quickly. Professional shelter staff take no risks of being bitten, have access to special equipment, and have years of experience handling and "reading" dogs. I had been trying to work a little with her self esteem, but the shelter environment was not ideal, and with the over-crowding problem, I asked if I could take her home after her stray time was completed. I thought perhaps in a quieter, less stressful setting she might just come around.

I knew our home was a little on the wild side, but still offered a better refuge. When we arrived home, I watched in amazement as she saw the kids getting out of the car. Her whole demeanor changed. She strained at the leash, jumping forward with her paws extended making a begging movement. Her body wiggled and jiggled with delight. This dog was clearly crazy about kids. Introductions were made and Ada was in heaven with these boys.

I don't recommend allowing children and new dogs to play unsupervised. I insisted that Ada wait in the crate until the dinner scene was over. She settled in and I was hopeful that maybe we could work with her confidence building process because of the positive feelings she had for children. She was comfortable around other dogs, although my dogs thought she was a bit of a looney tune getting so excited being with children.

She was extremely active, by far the fastest dog I had seen, and would race around our fenced yard by herself at "blur" speed. She seemed to take her cues from the kids. It appeared to me that she became familiar with my husband because the boys were at ease with him, so she followed their lead. I would bring my sons, Ben and Stewart, on walks with Ada and ask neighbors to come out and speak with our little group. I thought that with her "support" system in place, it would override her fears. It worked. My biggest problem was when I would open her crate, she would go absolutely wild. She would scream, race around, jump up and nip excitedly. I tried to make opening the crate uneventful by putting her in and opening it seconds later, quietly praising her if she didn't lose control. I started putting a leash on to avoid her running around and taught her to sit instead of jumping.

We were getting there, but it would take far more time and effort. Time that I didn't have. The shelter was at a point now where many dogs had been adopted via a promotional article in the newspaper. There were many good homes being offered and a golden opportunity that might not come again. I spoke with Barb and we agreed that after being in our home for three weeks, Ada should be brought back and put up for adoption. It was vital that I speak with any prospective adopters so they could continue her training, but also to explain what seemed to be working for her. I had written a story and put it on her cage, a general overview and summary, and the kind of home to which she would be best suited.

At first there were many inquiries, but nothing really serious or suitable. A few days later a family came in with, you guessed it, two boys and some experience with dogs under their belt, and they were in fact interested in Ada. Ada was a smaller dog, maybe 18 - 22 pounds, with a very sweet face and a stub for a tail. She had unfortunately reverted a bit, being back at the shelter, but at least we knew the potential and this behavior was temporary. It still broke my heart to see the panic back in her face, but she did recognize me as a friend which made it a little easier for her. The application from the family was a good one and I offered to take them for a walk with her. As predicted, she headed straight for the

children, which pleased the mom and dad. I explained about over-
stimulating situations and what she was capable of, and what I had
been working on. They felt they could handle that and continue
her training. I even offered to come over to their house if need be.
Papers were signed and Ada was on her way to a new life.

The mother phoned me a couple of times that week to complain
about the jumping and "hyper" activity. We talked at length about
proper exercise and the importance of the command "sit", among
other things. I offered to come over, but was assured everything
would be fine. Hearing nothing for about a week, I presumed the
situation was under control. In this business the saying: "No news
is good news" couldn't be more applicable!

It was about two weeks later when I came to work and saw Ada
pressed to the back of her cage with a return receipt on her cage.
The notation read: Reason for Return: son has allergies. Whether
or not it was true, I was disappointed to say the least, that they had
not called to notify me.

This was exactly what Ada didn't need, to be rejected yet again. I
felt guilty enough bringing her into my home and then
"abandoning" her, and now this plus only heaven and Ada knew
what had happened to her BEFORE her shelter entry. I called her
name and she did respond, wiggling over to the front of the cage. I
went inside the cage with her gave her a little massage and plunked
a kiss on the top of her head. It all seemed so unfair.

She went back up for adoption that day and again was applied for.
This time the application was from a younger couple who
explained that their life needed a dog. Both had grown up with and
still had dogs with parents, and now wanted one of their own.
Promises were made for training, exercising and socializing as Ada

once again left the building to start a new life. I vowed to myself to keep better tabs on her progress this time.

Day one went well with a nice walk in the park, and one tired girl. On day three, she broke out of her crate and chewed the carpet and molding around the door. The latch on the crate had not been fastened correctly, which explained her escape. Days turned into weeks and all seemed well, and I didn't want to make a nuisance of myself, although I had been told I was not an imposition.

About six weeks had passed, and I left a message on their machine saying I just called to chat and that I had pictures developed for them if they wanted a few. A few days later I still hadn't heard back so I left another short message. Maybe they were away, I thought, and decided to wait until my call was returned. It was really eating at me after ten days or so, when I finally called one evening from home and a tired voice answered. "I'm sorry to bother you, it's just Lorraine here calling to see how Ada is".

There was a long silence and for a minute I thought I had the wrong number or maybe I was going to be hung up on. At last the woman spoke. She began by telling me her "other half" had moved out leaving her with all the responsibilities of the dog, and with work and all...I knew something happened to Ada. I spoke too quickly. "Where's Ada?" I blurted. "Don't worry; we found her a good home" was her reply. I explained that a contract had been signed and if for any reason the adoption didn't work out the dog was supposed to be returned to the shelter. I felt my stomach go upside down. Where was dear Ada!?! I had to be a detective to find out everything I needed to know. I couldn't lose her or she would simply hang up and I may never find out.

She finally gave in and told me that she had been visiting her mother trying to sort out her life. Her mother lived in a small town quite a bit north of the city. She had taken Ada with her and she had "caused nothing but trouble" at her mom's house, so she dropped her off at the local shelter! My heart sank to my toes as I asked the name of the shelter and how long ago this took place. I didn't care if I had to drive 500 miles, I was going to find my darling Ada. She gave me the information I needed, but I knew I could not find out anything until the next day when the shelter opened. It was my day off, so I called right at 9:00 a.m. and asked to speak to the shelter manager and explained the story. She put me on hold while she looked up the information. Coming back on the line she said I would have to speak with her regional manager regarding the disposition of the dog because such matters were confidential. She gave me the number and I called and was put through to a voice mail system. I left a detailed message and asked him to return my call as soon as possible, which he did.

He explained in a kind voice that the dog in question was "aggressive", "impossible to handle by staff" and was "not suitable" for placement and had been put to sleep. I cried. I sat in my chair and wept for Ada. My whole body felt empty and hollow, completely drained.

Not all endings are fair or justified.   There are dogs in shelters across North America that die needlessly every day of every week and until society becomes more committed, responsible and educated, the useless killing of dogs will continue. There, I have said it. The truth is hard and cold, but I am not.

CHICLET

Shelter workers know and have seen things that are incomprehensible to most people. The abuse and neglect of children and animals is unforgivable, and such was the case of a five-pound Chihuahua named Chiclet. I have seen few sights as disgraceful as this with my own eyes. This tiny creature had just been brought in by an Inspector and cruelty charges were pending. His feet and legs exposed raw flesh, his toenails had curled three times around, making walking impossible, and his tail, obviously broken, lay hanging.

I stood staring at him in somewhat of a trance, which was interrupted by the shelter vet and the technician who had come in to examine him and prepare him for surgery. "What on earth happened?" I asked the technician. "We think he was dipped in some kind of acid!" she replied as she measured out the fluid in the syringe.

"Surely no one would do this intentionally," was all I could say. The look on her face told me otherwise. I turned to leave and get out of the way, when "I'll foster him" came blurting out of my mouth. She promised to let me know the outcome of the operation.

They were still working on him when my shift ended, so it wasn't until the next morning that I found out that his tail had to be amputated and some of his toes had literally disintegrated and fallen off during surgery. When I popped my head in to see him, he was sound asleep curled into a small ball. His back feet were wrapped with gauze as was his tail. It would be a while before he would be discharged. I figured that would give us time to become acquainted before I brought him home. He was certainly not ready for visitors yet, so the most I could do was talk to him through the bars and let him know someone cared.

Patience is the key.

Never force yourself on dogs.

The medical staff had to change his bandages daily and it was not going too smoothly. He was in a great deal of pain, as you might imagine, coming from such a dreadful situation, and his faith and trust in humans was nil. He was extremely difficult for the technicians to handle and medicate. Nancy, the head technician, asked if I might try to befriend him. I said I would try my best. Since I still had every intention of taking him home, it was important that I be able to touch him knowing I would have to continue some form of treatment.

I was a friend, a friend he didn't want. My heart always went out to the little dogs who were so frightened and rightly so. Imagine leading a life six inches off the ground in a world of giants... It would be pretty scary at the best of times. Everybody always bending over you, getting stepped on and constantly being picked up. I began by visiting him regularly and bringing him "special" tidbits. I spoke to him softly, told him funny stories, and sang goofy songs, hoping he would become accustomed to me and welcome my social calls.

I maintain that patience is the key. I do not like forcing myself on dogs and prefer to wait until they are ready and show willingness. I was making some strides, perhaps I should say "baby steps", which was better than going nowhere.

It was in his eyes. It always is. They would spark ever so slightly when I entered after about the third day. When it was time for his treatment his lips would rise, exposing every rotten little tooth in his head. I watched as the technicians were getting handling him down to a fine science. One would distract him while the other scooped him up wearing protective gloves. I hated seeing him stressed, but what else could be done when his recovery depended on this daily routine? It was on about the fifth day of working with him that the breakthrough I was waiting for came.

I had come to work early to see him, and as I approached his cage, he got up, his stubby wrapped tail actually moved, and his body invited me over. I opened the cage and put my hand down flat and left it there. Thus far, I had made no attempt to pat or touch him, just knowing the time hadn't been right. Now he was sniffing my hand and going into a play bow of sorts. Well, this was nice to see at long last. He was right at the edge of the cage now, and more out of reaction than good sense, I scooped him into my chest for fear of him falling. He made no attempt to scramble away; he looked rather pleased (and I sure was). So I decided to walk around and show him a few sights.

He seemed quite interested in the guided tour and snuggled a bit deeper into my body. I showed him our office and the lunch room. We were on our way to the ladies' room when I saw Nancy. She raised her eyebrows in surprise and nodded. "Finally!" was all she said. After our little adventure, I had to start work so I took him back to his "condo". I went to get him a clean blanket first, and when I went to put him back in this cage he put his two front paws on my shoulder. "Don't go now, the fun has just started!" I stroked his tiny body and put him on his blanket. As I left, he watched me go and behind the closed door I heard him start to whine a little. That, dear friends, was the beginning of a beautiful friendship, as the saying goes.

I received word that he was being released to foster care about three days later. I couldn't wait to get this darling home. He was going to be treated like a king! I was instructed how to clean and care for his healing wounds, and other than that he was in good shape, medically speaking.   He stayed in our home for approximately four weeks, and in that time grew to trust and accept the human race again. It always amazes me that the canine species is so forgiving!

I had an old borg type bear blanket that he claimed the first night and he used to cozy up into it, twirling and spinning around about 17 times before he would lay his head to rest. If it had to be washed, he would follow me downstairs and watch the procedure with a worried expression. He tried to settle but would continually run downstairs to check on his blanket. When it finally reappeared from the dryer, all warm and snugly, he would dance around and jump at my legs. He never "guarded" that old blanket, which he could have easily done.

I have seen a lot of dogs that growl and show their teeth over treasured possessions, but not Chiclet. If you watch children play, you will notice that it is the child who is unsure and afraid of losing that favorite toy that clings tightly to it and won't share. Kids that have been taught that sharing brings pleasure and friends to play with, will gladly "show off" their treasure and invite others to enjoy it with them. Many dog people may disagree with this analogy, stating there is a difference between dogs and children, and they are probably right to a point. However, I still maintain that there are many similarities. I realize that dogs do not have the same "reasoning" ability as people, but that just goes in the dog's favour, as far as I am concerned. There is no room for spite, revenge, and premeditated malice.

> **It always amazes me
> that the canine species is so forgiving!**

Dogs do make general and specific associations. However, I do not believe that dogs are out to get you, or to get even with you, or to purposely foil your plans. That is why the average pet dog owner needs so much education. If I had a dime for every time I heard the opening lines: "He did it out of spite", "She peed on the bed to get back at me", "He did it on purpose because I put him in his crate", "She knows better", "She chewed the drapes and couch because she's mad at me for going to work", and so on, I would be a rich but unhappy woman. All these comments refer to the dog as having powers beyond their realm, and sadly indicate that either there has been no effort made in teaching the dog, or all too often, the situation has been misdiagnosed leading to further confusion for the dog and frustration for the owner.

Chiclet's legs, feet and tail healed completely, and after a full examination by the shelter vet, he was given the approval for adoption. Every morning we had a taped message that stated what animals were ready for adoption that day and I put Chiclet on the recording. Opening time was 11:30, and at 10:30 I noticed an elderly lady already waiting patiently in the lobby. It wasn't until we opened for business that I found out she had traveled by bus and streetcar and had arrived early, and was in fact interested in seeing the five-year-old neutered male Chihuahua that was on the good morning tape. I directed her to the dog adoption room where Chiclet lay curled up on his fuzzy bear blanket. As she came out of the room, she asked where the applications were and wanted to fill out one for Chiclet. I reviewed the application myself and found her to be an excellent candidate!

After the interview was complete I revealed myself as the foster mother and told her of all he had been through. She listened intently, shaking her head in disgust at the description of his state when he arrived. I announced that I would go and get him out of the cage so she could meet him face to face. I brought him and his blanket snuggled closely, to the area where she was waiting. He was still a little uncertain of new people, or so I thought. He viewed her with keen interest and I placed him on the table.

Incredibly, and much to my surprise, he went right over to her and started sniffing her hand, and then the stub of a tail started to go. This introduction had proven to be very uplifting to say the least. I had to go into the office to get some literature, so I left the pair alone. In the office, everyone was interested to know if Chiclet was going home. I said in fact he was, and filled them in on the details, which took a minute. When I returned to the table there was Chiclet sitting in this woman's bosom! She explained that he had jumped into her blouse for warmth. He made no motion to leave his new found "comfort zone", and remained in her cleavage until we had finished the signing of the paperwork. She thought perhaps they should take a taxi home, so I called her one and I looked rather strange as I bent over to kiss the top of his head, with my face leaning into the lady's ample bust.

We spoke often at first, and then the phone calls became fewer and farther between. I did receive Christmas pictures of Chiclet in his Santa suit, and his new winter boots. He had a wardrobe that far exceeded my own, and the way I see it, no dog was more worthy of the luxuries that had been bestowed upon him.

Born in a cage
for science's sake
I'll live and die
No loving pat, no tender word for me.
A chain and a number
and daily fed until statistically
I've grown enough to die
"Three million animals used each year in Canadian labs."
I am a lab dog, one of these.
One of three million
scalded, poisoned, spinal crush,
blinded, drowned, lethal doses,
Which group test will I be?
I whimper unheard
and science is served.

- Author Unknown

ARCHIE

At six weeks of age, a Lab/Rottweiler mix was brought to the shelter with his left eye literally hanging out of the socket. Upon examination by the shelter vet, it was diagnosed that a severe blow to the side of the head had caused the injury. Working quickly, the puppy was prepped for an operation that would remove and seal the eye. Surgery at such a young age is always touch-and-go, and we hoped he would survive.

Barb, our shelter manager, approached me to ask if the pup made it through the operation, would I foster him? Without hesitation I replied, "Of course". All went well with surgery and provided no complications arose, arrangements were made for me to take the puppy home the following evening. That night as I prepared our home for his arrival, I explained to my boys that our new foster puppy would need much rest. He was not feeling well and needed to be quiet to get well. Whenever possible I like to set the ground rules before the animal comes home.

The next day, I checked with the head technician to see how "Archie" had fared the night. She was amazed at how well he had recovered and authorized his release that afternoon. As we drove home, Archie sat in his travel crate in the back seat looking around with his one remaining eye. His other eye had been sewn shut with five sutures. Even though I had been instructed to watch for any seeping from the stitched socket, it was not easy to look at his missing eye. Trying to imagine what this precious creature had been through was very difficult.

The first evening was uneventful. I fed him, and to my delight, his appetite had not suffered. He was very tired (and rightly so) and called it a day around 7:00 p.m.

I was involved at the time with another animal group in my community, which had a small shelter and needed volunteer help. Emily, their shelter supervisor, was an associate of mine and we spoke often. I caught up on a few phone calls, fed the little sleepyhead again and turned in. I had asked Gloria, my dear friend, savior, and neighbor, if she would mind attending to Archie while I was at work. I do not trust my dogs with many people; Gloria I trust. She is one of those neighbors who looks after your kids in a pinch, makes hot tea if you are home sick, or checks for the 47th time in case you might have left the stove on or the curling iron plugged in.

It wasn't until about three or four days after Archie arrived, that I received a strange phone call from Emily. A tiny, possibly deformed, six- to seven-week-old female lab mix had been brought into their shelter. She explained that the puppy's nostrils appeared to be blocked and they did not line up with the end of the muzzle. The young man who brought the pup in seemed to know nothing about her history and had made a quick exit. This puppy was to undergo surgery that evening to try and open the passages of her nose. "Abbey" (as Emily had named her) was in very serious trouble. We promised to stay in touch and say a prayer for dear Abbey.

True to her word, I heard from Emily the next morning to say the little soul had pulled through and she would take the puppy home herself. I had not had the opportunity to tell Emily about Archie yet, so I filled her in briefly about my new foster puppy. We joked about baby-sitting for each other - but to this day I don't know how we got on the subject of comparing notes about the origins of the two dogs.

One thing led to another, both parties did some checking, and lo and behold the addresses on both admittance receipts were the same, as was the name. "Good Lord!", I thought. The puppies were littermates! There are approximately 30 miles between the two shelters, and the street address was smack dab in the middle. I remember the chill that went up my spine when this information surfaced. Emily dispatched an inspector immediately and I ran to find Barbara. What was going on in that house?

Finally, the call from Emily came. The inspector reported that the address in question was indeed housing a litter of 6 Lab/Rottweiler puppies. The owner fit the description of the man Emily met 2 days previously. According to the owner the story goes like this: His purebred Rottweiler "bitch" was "knocked up" by a lab around the corner. One of the puppies (Abbey) was born deformed and the mother had attacked the other (Archie). He couldn't sell either one of them, so had taken them to local shelters to have them "disposed of."

The inspector investigated the premises and conditions in which the dogs were kept. Here is where animal work becomes difficult. Our idea of the way a dog should be kept and the standards set by the law are very different. "Adequate" shelter, food and water are the basic requirements, and they were provided in this situation. The mother and her puppies were being kept in the garden shed, which had been lined with straw, and a bowl of water was present. Having given the ever-famous speech about spay/neuter, and having tried to educate regarding the housing and care, the inspector had done all within her powers. We will never know what really happened to the two puppies before they came to us.

Knowing that we now had a brother/sister team, Emily and I made arrangements to reunite the pair, if the health of both puppies permitted. Two weeks later Archie's stitches had been removed, and Emily reported that Abbey was doing well; so I drove to Emily's flat with Archie. Now about eight weeks old, both puppies had been introduced to adult dogs, but had not had the luxury of being with other puppies. (I should take this time to let the readers know that both Abbey and Archie had been vaccinated to date, and neither was showing any symptoms of illness or this adventure would never have happened.) As we let them sniff each other, the tails started going a mile a minute and before we could say "Jack be Quick" they were into some "Doggy" game from which we were clearly excluded. "Archie the Hulk" was twice the size of petite Abbey, but other than size, they were unmistakably related.

I had recently attended a seminar given by Dr. Ian Dunbar and had applied all my new-found puppy knowledge to Archie. By the end of his foster stay he was well on his way to learning "sit", "down", and "come", and been obviously and positively introduced to children, dogs and cats. And I did host (quite honestly by accident) two "puppy parties".

Both dogs were due to go up for adoption that week, each at the shelter where they had been admitted. I always tried to bring my foster babies back on a Sunday because it was the best for adoptions. Also, I worked that day and had the opportunity to meet the people offering homes. I remember putting Archie in the dog adoption room that morning. His big black body with his Rottweiler head, and that one eye that looked at me as if to say "Hey, Mom, this is all wrong: I'm supposed to be out there with you", or "What the heck is going on around here; I'm with her, let me out!" Every single time I took a foster dog back to the shelter a piece of my heart went with them. I loved every one of them, but it is hard to explain to dogs that they each deserve a home of their own. A place to call "mine"; a family for just "me". For some, our foster home was the best thing that had ever happened to them, despite the competition.

Getting back to the story, Archie was now up for adoption and all the potential families were in the room looking. I was sidetracked as usual about something or other and Eileen, my adoption co-worker, whispered to me that she had just taken an application from a young couple who wanted Archie. "Let me know", I said (which meant if the home was good then I'd go out and introduce myself; which is exactly what happened).

"Hello, my name is Lorraine, I'm Archie's foster mother". I looked at the young couple, who were smiling at me anxiously. We got comfortable at the table and got to know each other. I think back and wonder if some of these people thought I was crazy. When you take a dog into your home to nurture and care for, I doubt if most people have any idea of what you have gone through. My emotions were always in overdrive.

A few minutes into the conversation, I knew they were the right home for Archie. In this business you listen to your gut. Listening and exchanging stories, knowing that soon Archie would be with his new family, I was excited for him. All was said and done, and I gathered the dopey black lug into my arms for the last time as I took him to the lobby where they were waiting. Promising pictures and letters, the couple waved good bye as Archie's one eye looked around in excitement at the prospect of a new adventure. "Maybe a 'Doggy' game with that young filly I met last week, a game of ball perhaps, or it must be time to pee." I tried to read his mind. "No, buddy - it's time for you to go home".

True to their word, they sent me a whole roll of photographs, and at Christmas sent me a card with more photos tucked inside. The last note I received was to tell me they were tired of city living and had purchased a home north of the city. Archie was 109 pounds and now had another sister, a nine-month-old black cat who had come from the shelter near their new home. Enclosed was a picture of the two of them, dog and cat stretched out on the bed together.

Abbey was just as lucky, although I cannot fill you in with such detail. Emily called about a week after Archie had been adopted to tell me a family had come in for Abbey. I was lucky enough to visit the shelter where Emily worked one day when a young lab mix dragged in a rather embarrassed, but happy looking woman. "Abbey, Abbey," Emily screamed from behind the counter. She looked terrific. As Emily and Abbey had a "love in" reunion, the woman sang the praises of her precious pet. Abbey was six months old then and had come in for a visit and a spay. I thought it appropriate that I leave and let the three of them have their time together.

DANA

Other than our two family dogs, who both lived past 11 years, Lacey was the only dog I had lost personally. Her loss had left our home with a hollow empty void. As if her death wasn't enough, nothing could have prepared me for what was ahead.

Ian and I had discussed the idea of adopting another dog, and had agreed that if I met a dog that I felt would enjoy living in a nut house we would open up our hearts and home. Working with homeless dogs and knowing you can't adopt one is hard, but knowing you can is even harder! Every face I saw was a potential.

We wanted a large dog and 90% of the dogs in the shelter were large. Because I am always attracted to the older dogs, my first choice was an eight- to ten-year-old German shepherd named Dino. I had been working with Dino for a few days, and trying desperately, without success, to cheer him up. I would take him out for walks and try and jolly him along without the slightest hint of even a tail wag. We used to sit in the office together and I would gently stroke his gray muzzle and tell him stories of days gone by.

Dino and I were having lunch together when one of the veterinarians from the clinic stopped to chat with us. He stroked Dino's grand head and stopped short under his ear. "He's got a growth here," he remarked as he bent down to check further. He then commented on his poor condition and lack of muscle in his hindquarters. "Poor old guy, he's certainly got his problems" he stated. I remarked that I was considering adopting this old fellow. The veterinarian smiled warmly at us but shook his head doubtfully. "It's hard to say without a proper look, but I think the reason you are having trouble cheering him up is because he's probably in pain." I felt just awful. Here I was lugging this poor old dog around who would have been just as happy to be left in peace. I should have thought to read his medical sheet more carefully and not been so selfish. I put him back in his cage and watched as he plunked his tired body down on his quilt.

Later that afternoon I went to check on Dino and there he lay in his own feces, unable to get up. I knew now that what the veterinarian had said was true. His old body didn't have enough energy or strength to remove himself from the excrement. The decision was made to free Dino of his suffering. I stayed and held him, and tried to comfort him while his pain slipped away. I was still grieving the death of Lacey and now as I held dear Dino, all my wounds were reopened.

Two weeks later as I walked around the kennels I immediately noticed the two timid shepherd mixes in the same cage. They must have been found together, as we normally do not double up dogs. One of the dogs had huge erect ears and a compact body; the other was larger with drop ears. Both had shepherd faces and were black and tan. I read the receipts which indicated the dogs had been abandoned in an old warehouse downtown.

Does it ever cease to amaze you how irresponsible and insensitive people can be? For every story I tell you, there are hundreds, even thousands that are not told. Right away I knew these dogs would never be claimed. They had been deliberately left behind. Both dogs had their bodies pressed to the back of the cage, eyes wide with fear, each trying to hide behind the other. I continued to read the paperwork. One was a female and one was a male, probably littermates, most likely obtained as "guard" dogs for the warehouse. They had yet to be aged, but looked young. As I was observing the dogs I was approached by one of the women who worked in the kennels.

"They need some work, socially speaking, but something tells me they have great potential," she admitted. "How about you work with one and I'll work with the other and see what we can do?" I asked. She was readily agreeable. It was decided that I would work with the female I called "Miss Giant Satellite Ears".

When two scared dogs are in the same cage, two philosophies can be argued. One is that at least they have each other for company. The second is that they feed off of each other's fears. If our suspicions were right and these two dogs were littermates, that would mean they had developed an extremely strong bond, coupled with the fact that they had probably not received much human companionship. We came to the difficult decision that it would be in their best interest to separate them, cage-wise, but allow them visiting time.

If we had any hope of finding them homes, we would have to gain their trust, and we needed to get to know them as individuals. To be realistic, not many adopters come to the shelter and ask if we have two large dogs who would like a home together, so we knew it was most likely that they would eventually have to be separated. My charge, "Dana", was a shy, easily frightened girl who started showing signs of improvement daily. I earned her trust early in the relationship and she eagerly approached the front of her cage now when she heard my voice. I had the technician look her over and it was estimated that she was about two years old and in good physical condition. Her brother, as I will call him, was in good shape also. I enjoyed taking Dana out for walks and watched as she rediscovered herself.

Once, while on one of our walks, a mother and two children were getting out of their car to visit the shelter. At the sight of the two children, Dana's demeanor softened, her tail started to wag, and she pulled toward them. She flattered me by making it clear that she was my girl. Her large brown eyes looked up into my face as I spoke and even when I didn't. I felt without doubt that this was the dog I wanted to bring home to my family, especially after seeing her reaction to the two children.

However, my excitement came to a shuddering halt when the clinic veterinarian came over to the shelter to inform the staff that an outbreak of parvovirus had hit our city. Local veterinarians had called to warn him about the high number of positive cases they were seeing. He also informed us it was quite possible that there were dogs in the shelter harbouring the virus.

Parvovirus is a highly contagious, often deadly virus. "Parvo" is a shelter's worse nightmare and, if not contained quickly and effectively, can infect the entire shelter within a matter of days. Hot weather seems to provide perfect conditions for parvovirus. Puppies and geriatric dogs tend to be more at risk, but healthy adult dogs are by no means immune. The symptoms consisted of vomiting, diarrhea (especially bloody), and lethargy. The shelter had purchased a kit that could test the stool of "possible" cases.

Our nightmare began with a 10-week-old puppy who had come in as a stray. The tell-tale signs were present and after testing the stool, it was confirmed that this young pup was infected with parvovirus. Staff worked quickly to bleach every inch of space that the pup had contacted, and more. At the time, the only solution we knew of that would kill the deadly virus was a proper mixture of chlorine bleach and water.

It is very difficult to explain how these infected dogs suffer. You can literally smell death permeating their bodies. If the virus is diagnosed from the onset, a veterinarian can hook the dog up to I.V. fluids immediately and the chances of survival are much higher than a dog that has become symptomatic and receives post treatment. Unfortunately, the shelter was dealing with the latter, and in the case of the puppy, he was so far gone the kindest thing we could do for him was to end his pain and suffering by having him euthanized. We were to find out that this was only the beginning of what was the worst parvo summer in history.

We were given strict orders that no dogs were to be "socialized" until further notice. Each day for over a week we would have anywhere from two to five positive parvo readings. The saddest part was that most were puppies whose lives had not even begun and were being ended. This took quite a toll on the staff and we were all emotionally and physically drained. Despite the horror, the medical staff was remarkable. At the first sign of vomiting or diarrhea, they would quickly isolate the dog and collect the sample for testing. They were running on empty but persevered to try and prevent an epidemic. However, the situation became so serious that we closed adoptions and spent hours bleaching and disinfecting cages. We put out press releases to all the newspapers to alert the public. We let people know how vital it was to vaccinate their dogs and puppies and to avoid taking puppies to frequently visited "dog" parks. Things finally started to look up again after several days passed with no new signs of the illness.

Dana's stray time was finally over, and I was ready to take her home. I went home for lunch that day to check on something, and returned to work an hour later in anticipation. I would take Dana home at 4:00. I passed several staff members in the hall and received some strange looks, but I was too excited to see Dana to worry about it. As I rounded the corner, I bumped right into Nancy, our head technician. "I'm all ready for my new baby!" I boasted. Just the look on Nancy's face told me instantly that something had gone wrong in the last hour. "What's wrong?" I questioned. She indicated that we should speak in private. Nancy broke the news. "While you were at lunch Dana broke with diarrhea, we tested the stool, and I'm sorry Lorraine, but Dana has Parvo". She continued, "We have isolated her, she is in the infirmary. I have to speak with Barbara to see what it is she wants to do now".

I just stood there in complete shock. I couldn't believe my ears. I realized immediately what the situation was. I couldn't even consider the possibility of having her treated at the shelter. It wasn't fair to the other dogs to try and save one dog while there were hundreds that were at risk. But I just knew in my heart that if she could get treated she would make it. She was otherwise a strong healthy adult dog and the chances of her surviving were high.

I ran to the office and called my private veterinarian. Maybe I could take her there and have him take care of her. The answer I got was what I had anticipated. "I'm sorry Lorraine, but I cannot risk it. I have dogs in and out of here, and besides I do not have the facilities for added isolation," he explained. I couldn't blame him. How could I ask him to put his practice in jeopardy? Had I not been so desperate, I would have felt guilty just asking him.

I saw Barb coming down the hall and knew what she was going to say. Dana was going to have to be put to sleep. I just couldn't deal with any more death; my whole body was shutting down. Barbara motioned to me and we walked down the hall together. "I know you want this dog, and I am going to set up a mini-quarantine room. We have just tested two more young adult dogs and both had positive parvo readings. All three dogs have greater than average chances of pulling through, the vet said, and quite frankly, I am tired of euthanizing dogs this week. I just can't do it anymore".

I listened in amazement to her plan. I wanted to hug her and throw her up in the air, but I contained myself. "The only people allowed in the room will be one technician and one kennel attendant. They will be fully robed in disposable protective gowns. Nancy will orchestrate the medical aspect. All dogs will be put on I.V. within the hour." I thanked her for going the extra mile. I found out later that afternoon that one of the other parvo dogs was also spoken for by one of the summer students. The room that housed the dogs was at the back of the building in a low-traffic area, and there were two large windows that the technicians could look through without having to go in if need be.

Thinking I was coming home with this dog, I had been talking about her for over a week. I now had to explain to Ian and the boys that Dana was sick and we would have to wait until she got better before she could come home. It was my day off the next day, so I called the shelter to ask how Dana was doing. The report I received was that she was holding her own. She would make it, I just knew it.

Later that evening I got a call from the night technician. "Dana is not doing very well, Lorraine. She can't seem to lift her head and is pretty flat out. I think you should come down and be with her, just in case, well, you know, in case she starts to go downhill". I grabbed my car keys, yelled something to Ian and drove down to the shelter.

I caught up with the night technician and she handed me a disposable gown and latex gloves. "I really thought this dog was going to make it," I told the tech as she helped me tie the strings of the gown. "She may yet; we'll know in the next 24 hours. I just figured you may want to see her, and maybe you could cheer her up," the technician responded. "She's probably forgotten me, I haven't been able to interact with her for a while, but I will be sure to tell her she has a nice home waiting for her," I said. I saw her from the window. As I entered the room, there was not the normal loud greeting of barking and jumping. I approached her cage and opened the gate. I spoke in a quiet gentle tone and reached over to touch her head.

Before I could speak another word, she leapt up, knocked the water bowl upside down, danced and wiggled, licked my face and hands, and wrapped the I.V. line around my neck. I had not expected this. I looked over, and through the window I could see the technician waving and holding her thumb up. "You are supposed to be flat out, you big goof!" I grabbed Dana's long muzzle and frisked her around in a playful game. I had to be careful; she was still hooked up to the intravenous. I spent some time with her and then as she calmed, I decided to leave and let her get some rest. The technician asked if I would mind seeing if she would eat the food she had prepared. I took the bowl of special food into Dana and she finished it in a blink. We were both pleased with what we had seen and by then we both knew she was going to make it!

A few days later the waiting game was over, and all three dogs had survived parvo - a milestone for the shelter. The other good news was that not one other dog had come down with the deadly virus. "We did it! We did it!" I wanted to shout from the rooftops. It had been a revival for the staff and a long overdue success story.

In the event a dog survives parvo, the stool must be checked to ensure the virus is still not shedding itself through the feces. After a negative reading is produced that dog is not contagious. Samples were collected from the three dogs and sent to the lab. Of course the only one that came back positive was Dana's, but that was fine, at least the one dog had a home to go to and the other fellow could go into adoption. It was just a matter of time before Dana was clear. Do you know that darn dog did not have a poop for three days!??! Nobody could believe it. Finally, when it came I felt like throwing a party! Needless to say it was negative, but I was at home when the results came in, so I asked my son Ben if he felt like going to the shelter and picking up Dana. "Hooray" he responded with enthusiasm.

We drove down together chatting the whole way about what fun we were going to have with our new friend. When we arrived, the shelter staff greeted us sharing in our excitement. "Come on Ben, I'll show you where Dana is," I said, taking his little hand. I took him with me to look through the glass window. She was the only dog in there now, so it wasn't hard to know that she was the one.

Her big ears shot forward at the sound of voices outside the door. "Hey look mom, she looks like a deer with those ears!" Ben pointed. "I'll go in and get her and bring her out to meet you. I'll be right back," I instructed Ben. I slipped the leash over her neck as she jumped and twirled.

During our ride down to the shelter I had reminded Ben how to introduce ourselves to new dogs. He was standing still and was ready so I allowed Dana to sniff him. She was clearly very happy with this little person, so I told Ben he could just put a hand forward. As he did this, her head plunked in it anticipating a chin scratch. He giggled and I let him know it was fine to stroke her gently, but not to try and hug or kiss her. "Can we go home now, Mom? I want to show her our house." "Sure, let's head out," I agreed. As we were walking along the back hall, Dana was nearly out of her skin. I waved our good byes to the staff and headed for our car.

On the drive home I arranged it so that Ben was in the front seat with me and Dana had the back seat to herself. We had an old wagon at that time and she kept flipping over the seat to the trunk area and back. She sure was a dramatic change from old Lacey who sat gracefully in the car looking out the window. I must not compare, I kept reminding myself, but it is human nature to do so, at least at the beginning.

We arrived home to meet the troops. I still had Dana on the leash as I walked into the house. It was not the introduction I was hoping for or would recommend. Ben was talking in his loudest voice, Bingo, Chico and Miss Penny thought the house was being raided, and Stewart was trying to squirm out of Ian's arms. "Let's try and keep things down to a dull roar," Ian smiled, trying to calm the situation. "I'll take the canine half out to the backyard," I said, as Ben followed. "Last time I checked you were not a dog, Ben," I joked. "Please Mom, I'll stay out of the way," he pleaded. I said he could come as long as he stayed by my side and let the dogs do their thing. Dana was the perfect lady as she allowed herself to be examined by the senior citizens from head to toe. I presumed she passed inspection as everyone was now doing his or her own thing and was happy. We took them back into the house and I explained that if we could try to settle down and be calm, Dana would hopefully do the same.

WRONG! She was so darned excited she couldn't stay still for more than a minute. She paced, panted and whined. I brought our crate up from the basement and put it in the bedroom for Dana to sleep in. After the kids were in bed, I took Dana for a walk around the neighbourhood with Bingo. I was so exhausted from the day's events I just wanted to hit the hay. I put some treats in the crate and let Dana go in and get them, leaving the door open. I knew I should introduce the crate more slowly and was expecting too much by asking her to spend the night there. Our house was not one that could be easily cordoned off, and I did not want her having the run of the house all night. Thankfully, after a few in and outs with the crate, she was getting pretty comfortable with it. At the shelter she had been confined to her cage, so this was not entirely a new concept. She did fairly well and after a little whining fell into a deep sleep.

The next morning she had been recharged and I had quite the fireball on my hands. It took us no time at all to realize that her love for children was a gift far greater than we had ever expected. We had one major problem: housetraining was non-existent. If she had to go she would simply take care of the matter regardless of where she was. I would accompany her to the toilet area and await results. If there were none, I would bring her back in and either crate her or tie her to me for 10 or 15 minutes and then offer the toilet area again. I was convinced this dog had a bladder the size of the Good Year Blimp! When I finally got results I praised and fussed over her like no other dog I have ever had. But just when I thought I had an empty bowel and bladder, allowing her some freedom, I would find "surprises" in the basement. I would just have to watch her more closely, I figured, even if it meant gluing myself to her. I took the bowel movement from the basement and put it outside where I wanted her to relieve herself, thinking if she smelled herself outside it might help matters.

I never scolded or shamed her for my findings. After about two weeks of keeping my eye on her, offering the desired area often, and praising her for outdoor elimination, her housetraining habits were in place. Having that little problem out of the way was a relief.

We walked the same route each day, but one morning we had a setback of sorts. We were walking by my neighbour's house where a large German shepherd named Princess resides. Princess makes no bones about the fact that she takes "guarding" her home seriously. Now don't get me wrong. Princess is not a guard dog per se; she is a housedog, a family pet and a very nice dog. In fact, I know Princess very well as I babysat for the folks when they went away. I would say that when Princess is alone in her home it would not be a wise thought to consider entering. This one particular day, Dana and I were on our way to the park via Princess' house and as we approached, out of the side door bolts Princess. Before I had time to react, Dana had been rolled and lay on her back with all four legs in the air! Princess stood over her with a satisfied look, almost a grin. My neighbour came running out in her pajamas, apologizing profusely, calling her dog's name. Hearing her name, Princess immediately left the scene at hand and ran over to my neighbour, wagging her tail.

Dana did not forget that frightful day. The next outing proved the point. As we approached the "scary" house, Dana's hackles rose and from the depths of her soul came a sound I had never before heard. Barking and lunging at the end of the leash, she targeted that house. She was ready this time, no more surprise attacks. Now I had to think of a way to counteract this situation. Unfortunately, I was getting this behaviour now when ANY dog was in sight. I had to use every bit of brainpower I had to solve this one. My first problem was that she is stronger than I am, so I could hardly hang on to her when this reaction happened. I purchased a head collar and that proved invaluable. I now had control of her head, which leads the body.

I used praise and hot dogs when she did not react and neighbours used to see me dancing and singing down the street just to keep Dana focused on what I was doing! I practiced sits and stays and "watch me" eye contacts at home and other easier locations before trying to use them in a high-distraction situation. She has come a long way; however, to this day if she is caught off-guard by another dog, her reaction is still one of full hackles and barking. I can gain control quickly, by a variety of requests including "sit", "quiet please", "leave them", "don't bother", or some fancy heeling. The most ironic part is that there is not a kinder, more gentle, tolerant dog than Dana when it comes to the canine species. She has helped me raise foster puppies (some only 4 weeks old!) and put up with old grumps and numerous adult foster dogs from the shelter.

As mentioned previously, Dana's deep trust and affection with children was evident from day one. If her behaviour had been evaluated in the shelter environment, it would have been impossible to predict her true temperament. Although her timidness with men was displayed in the shelter and continued in the "real world", she overcame that weakness one man at a time.

Each introduction becomes easier. It is with my son Ben that I am most proud. The two have a special and often secret friendship, one that is sometimes only dreamed of. The familiar smiling face and wagging tail that greets him daily brightens a bad day at school. I watch with awe as Ben whispers sweet nothings into her rabbit ears, Dana absorbed by every word. At the sound of his voice her eyes light up, head cocked awaiting their next adventure, following his every step. His projects at school often reflect his deep relationship with his trusted dog Dana. He is learning that animals are living, feeling and loving creatures who should be treated with respect and compassion, and for this I am grateful.

Through all the pain and death I had to deal with that summer of 1993, I have to say that in spite of all the problems, Dana emerged as our "Knight In Shining Armor".

CHARLIE

"Surely an eight-week-old puppy can't be in quarantine for biting!" Barbara complained as she looked at the paperwork on her desk. I was in her office for a regular weekly meeting, which always included, among other things, lengthy discussions about the animals in the adoption area. "Maybe it's a mistake," I ventured, assuming it was puppy biting. If not schooled in the fine art of gentleness, some puppies can get carried away and chomp down pretty darn hard. "Well, let's go and see this little monster," Barbara said as she got up.

We headed towards the "observation" room, went in, and there he was. A deep rich red wrinkled face looked up at us, his body dancing in excitement at the sight of visitors. He had the look of a chow chow, only with short bristled hair. He jumped and wiggled, extending a paw in hopes of one of us taking it. We decided to investigate this report further, and find out all the details which had led this puppy here.

We had never before had such a young dog admitted into this area. If a dog bite occurs, it is the responsibility of the owner to have the dog quarantined for between 10 and 14 days. This can be done at home if the Health Department permits, or is done at a facility such as a shelter or Animal Control building. If the dog is a stray and bites someone, the animal agent will take the report from the bitten party and automatically place the dog in the observation area.

We were curious to know more about this puppy. What we did find out was a bit surprising. The owner gave us all the information we needed to know. The mother had been hit by a car when the puppies were three or four weeks old. All the puppies had died except this one. The owner had been feeding the puppy a mixture of skim milk and crushed dog biscuits. She had always had "trouble" feeding the puppy as he would attack the food and her hand if it came too close. He had constant diarrhea, and she didn't want him anyway. So, since the starving puppy had grabbed her hand (and broken skin) while eating, she had insisted he be quarantined for rabies! What is wrong, besides everything, with this picture?

After hearing the story, we both knew this puppy deserved a break. My assignment was to take him home, observe him, and work with him if needed, after the ten-day holding time. It just happened by chance that I was scheduled to clean and feed the room he was in for most of the week. You could tell by the way he devoured his food that he had been malnourished. Now that he was on a regular schedule and a good diet, hopefully his diarrhea would clear up and in time he would cease consuming each meal as if it were his last. Immediately I noted that he growled as he ate. Considering the circumstances I was not overly surprised; however, I hoped that when I had him home his manners could be improved.

His ten-day quarantine period proved what we already knew, that he did not have rabies. He had grown considerably in the week and a half, and his deep auburn coat shimmered in the sunlight as I loaded him into my car. He was one handsome puppy. The extra folds of skin hung loosely around his neck and framed his head like that of a young lion cub. I decided to call him Charlie, not an overly exciting name for such a dignified looking fellow, but I liked the sound of Charlie the Chow Chow, and since I have a tendency to sing to my dogs I felt I could jingle out a pretty good tune using these words.

Using the technique I learned from my Ian Dunbar seminars, I began our "food bowl" work. I placed the empty food dish down and was met with a look of bewilderment. I added a few kernels of the puppy chow which were immediately inhaled. I repeated this several times, always waiting until he had finished before continuing. There had been no growling up to this point, and I made sure I praised him for just that. Nearing the end of the meal, I had the last of the kibbles in my hand for depositing. He was just finishing up and still had his head in the dish. As I reached my hand closer to the dish, he growled and snapped. He was so far off the target of my hand, I had to wonder if he really meant to connect.

My reaction to his snap was pretty simple. The kibble in my hand that was going to be his was put back in the jar on the kitchen counter. End of supper. No hitting, rolling over, yelling, or staring. It was quite amusing actually to see the look on his dear face. Each day we went through the same ritual, and each day we made progress. His diarrhea problem came and went and I reported this to the shelter veterinarian, who asked me to bring in a sample. This I did, and all showed normal. We carried on with our food bowl work. We had a few more growling episodes, but the snapping had disappeared. We had also done all the other fun puppy things which include "pass the puppy", "sit", "down" and "come". By the end of his stay, which was about two weeks, he had become a perfect gentleman. I was very proud of his progress.

Pass the puppy, for those of you who may be wondering, is another Ian Dunbar idea; a marvelous socializing exercise. This activity involves introducing the puppy to children in a gentle, fun and kind manner. By having children touch and handle the young dog, giving treats, giggles and other positive reinforcers, the pup soon associates kids with pleasantries and is comfortable and confident in the company of youngsters. I always made a point of telling childless couples who were adopting puppies this information asking them to "borrow" a neighbourhood or relative child.

Charlie was at ease with children, having been in close contact with our two boys for the past two weeks, and was also interacting with our resident dogs, as did all our foster dogs.

When I took him back to work to put him up for adoption, everyone was happy to see and hear of all his achievements. His stools had been consistently firm so he was put into adoption that day. I was not expecting the interest that he was generating. Unfortunately, it seemed that his breed was attracting people who wanted to either use him as a guard/garage dog, or wanted him to (believe it or not, in this day and age!) BREED! It was extremely frustrating.

As I sat in the office filing, an old familiar face popped a head in the doorway. "Hey, long time no see!" the young man smiled. His name was Jeff and we had gone to high school together. Although he and I were a few years apart (me being the elder!) our parents' homes were only blocks away from each other. Jeff was, in fact, a good friend of a friend of mine. We reminisced about days gone by while I continued to file. I asked him what brought him down to the shelter. He explained that he lived not far from the shelter and had come down to visit the animals. What he said next nearly knocked me off my chair. "We have a spayed female chow chow at home and I thought maybe she might like a friend," he casually mentioned. "Have you been in to see the dogs yet?" I asked. "I'm going in to take a look now," Jeff said. I had a funny feeling he hadn't seen my Charlie boy yet, as I'm sure he would have inquired. It would be a dream come true if Jeff was interested. Minutes later, he reappeared asking if Charlie was still available.

I wanted to look over my shoulder to see if a guardian angel was setting this up. I told him that Charlie was in need of a good home, and I was his foster mom. I explained in great detail the history of this puppy and what I had been doing at my home. Jeff assured me that he would continue the approach I had taken and also had experience with Sasha, his Chow Chow. He wanted to speak to his roommate first and have him come down and see the puppy. He said he could have it all arranged within a couple of hours. My shift was coming to an end so I told him to speak with my co worker Emily, when he returned later that evening. He filled out the necessary forms which were all in order, and promised not to be too long.

I left for home, but not before giving Charlie a big kiss, and asked Emily to call me and let me know how things worked out with Jeff and his roommate. The call came shortly after 6:00 PM. Jeff had adopted Charlie and they were at the pet supply shop stocking up. I asked Emily to run out and give Jeff my home phone number so we could keep in touch. I was so glad that Charlie and Jeff had found each other.

A week hadn't gone by when I got a message to call Jeff. I was hoping against hope that Charlie had not reverted with the growling around the food bowl. When I called back Jeff explained that Charlie was experiencing some diarrhea and he had taken him to his private veterinarian, who wanted to do some tests. I told him that I had some trouble also, but it had cleared up and the stool check that we had done was negative for parasites. Jeff felt he wanted to go ahead with the tests and was just letting me know. I asked how everything else was going and he told me things were great. The two dogs got along well, he had experienced no trouble with the food dish, and in fact, other than the diarrhea, Charlie was adjusting fine and loved all. That part I was delighted to hear. I felt sure his medical condition would be taken care of and overcome.

A month or so went by and I decided to call and invite myself over for tea. They lived within walking distance so I could scoot over on my lunch hour with time to spare. Jeff was excited to hear from me and we made arrangements to have lunch that very week. They had a beautiful home. It was an old house that had been renovated into a modern multi-level dwelling while keeping the old fashion charm. As I entered the back door, both dogs came bounding out to see who had come to visit.

Charlie looked magnificent. He had grown into a wonderful happy creature who resembled a bear whose skin was too big for his body. Sasha did not share Charlie's enthusiasm at my intrusion, but was not impolite. I ate the lunch that Jeff had so kindly made for me, and we chatted until my time ran out. I had asked about

Charlie's diarrhea; Jeff said the veterinarian had prescribed some medication and changed the diet and all seemed under control. We said our good-byes and promised each other to stay in touch. As I walked back to work, I felt a deep sense of satisfaction and contentment. I let my mind wander and day dream about how nice it would be if all the animals had proper, loving homes, and how glad I would be if someday I was out of job.

It was about four months later when I heard from Jeff again. Charlie's diarrhea was back in a big way and his vet had recommended a specialist. Jeff let me know that Charlie was scheduled for an exploratory scope the next week with the top veterinarians in the field. He would take Charlie there, about a two hour drive, and would let me know what the diagnosis was. I could think of little else for the duration.

The call came the day of the surgery. The second I picked up the phone and heard Jeff's voice I knew the news was not good, but I had never expected to hear what Jeff had to say. The results of the scope had shown that the tissue damage to Charlie's bowels were "the worst" the veterinarian had ever seen. While Charlie was still under the anesthetic the doctors had called Jeff and explained that the situation offered little or no hope, in their expert opinion. Jeff had authorized the euthanasia then and there to end Charlie's suffering. Charlie never woke up that day.

Jeff and I cried together for that dear soul, who, at eight months would never again run and play with his friend Sasha, would not grow old and tired surrounded by the love of his family, and would never again feel the sun shine on his deep auburn coat.

I wish someone would tell me, what it is that I've done wrong?
Why do I have to stay chained up and left alone so long,
They seemed so glad to have me when I came here as a pup,
There were so many things we'd do while I was growing up.

The master said he'd train me as a companion and a friend
The mistress said she'd never fear to be alone again,
The children said they'd feed me and brush me every day
They'd play with me and walk me, if I would only stay.

But now the master "hasn't time", the mistress says I shed
She doesn't want me in the house, not even to be fed,
The children never walk me, they always say "not now"
I wish that I could please them, won't someone tell me how?

All I had, you see, was love, I wish they would explain
Why they said they wanted me, and then left me on a chain?

- Edith Lassen Johnson

RICKY

Ricky was a chubby old Chihuahua with a fractured front leg who needed a foster home until the leg healed. As you have noticed, I really have a soft spot for small dogs and especially Chihuahuas. Ricky, as I named him, was tri-coloured, neutered and about 10 years old. And to put it politely, a tad chunky. I offered to foster him right away. The healing time, the vet figured, was anywhere from six to eight weeks. The medical staff had put a splint on his leg that was to be changed on schedule, and he was to remain in the crate, except for relieving himself.

I was getting him ready to go home when he lifted his leg in the hallway outside our office. I turned to get a paper towel and noticed he had blood in his urine. Back to the medical staff I went to report my findings. As I walked along, Ricky kept stopping and trying to urinate, but now nothing was coming out. Dr. Campbell was still in the examination office and I explained what I had just witnessed. I was asked to bring in a urine sample the next day, but Ricky could still go home with me.

If it wasn't one thing it was another. Poor old guy. Things were bad enough having a fractured leg, now he had some kind of urinary problem. Well, lucky for him, we noticed it right away. When we arrived home I set up his luxury style-crate with soft quilts. After taking him out for a bowel movement, which he produced, I popped him in his crate. I would get the sample in the morning with a little tray of some sort and then put it into the container I had been given. He was as quiet as a church mouse. I forgot he was there and when Ian came home he asked who our latest visitor was. I carried him to the backyard frequently, knowing he must be uncomfortable with his infection.

The next morning I collected the urine that needed to be tested. I could see blood through the clear jar. I handed it in as soon as I got to work, so the technicians could send it off to the lab. The results would take a day or so. That evening I held him on my lap while we watched some T.V. He was the sweetest dog. His face was so alert, he did not impose on my dogs, and actually he took quite a fancy to Miss Penny. She was quite a hot number with the wild hair-do she was sporting lately. Chico didn't like him (but then Chico doesn't like anybody of any species), but Ricky took no personal offense.

The next morning the test results were in and they were not very good. Ricky had crystals in his urine and had to be on a special diet along with a prescription. I followed the instructions to the letter, but still he did not improve. His leg was healing well, but Dr. Campbell was not happy that Ricky was not responding to the urinary treatment. The second urine sample showed little or no improvement.

Dr. Campbell called me into his office late one afternoon to explain the results and what our options were. He said that although it was a little risky, he did recommend that Ricky have surgery. By doing the operation he would unblock the passage and force the crystals out. Apparently, this operation is much more common in male cats, often with excellent results. My only reservation was that Ricky was a 10 year old dog and may not take to the anesthetic well. But if it would free him from the pain forever, it would be worth it. We spoke to Barbara and all agreed that it was the right move.

Surgery was scheduled for the very next day. No food or water past midnight. I spent that night cuddling Ricky and telling him that he was the best darn dog on earth. My dogs were not overly impressed by the attention being lavished on this overweight freeloader, but they were always tolerant. I thought if dear Ricky didn't wake up, or something went wrong, at least he would know how much I loved him.

When the surgery began, Nancy, the head technician, said it was a lengthy procedure and not to worry. I would of course worry, but I would not bother them. It seemed like days before Nancy's voice paged me over the intercom. I ran in to see how he had done. He was still asleep, and wrapped in a blanket. Dr. Campbell's explanation compared Ricky's urinary tract to old corroded pipes.

The walls were literally thick with debris and it was no wonder the urine could not pass through. Nancy touched my arm lightly and leaned over, "We lost him once, but we got him back. He had a really rough go of it, Lorraine." Dr. Campbell looked like he was glad it was over.

I obviously couldn't take him home that day. In fact, he was pretty much out of it for the next two or three days. On day four Nancy said he was in good spirits and could go out to relieve himself. This was the big test!

I was taking him out the back door to the grassy area, only we didn't make it that far. He took about 10 steps and let her rip. A giant puddle formed on the floor. There was no blood, and he did not stop until he was finished. I bet he felt like a million bucks! I was given the word that he could come home with me that night. He was so full of beans, and that was sure nice to see.

After about two weeks, tests were done again, and he passed with flying colours. His leg had long since healed, and now it was time to think about his future. His time had come to be adopted. As always, I wrote a story about what he had been through and how wonderful he was. He would need a special diet to prevent any reoccurrence. I guess when people read the story they didn't want to take on what they perceived as a "problem", or maybe it was because he was 10 years old.

It had been a week and still no one was showing any interest. In the office the phones were always ringing with inquiries about the animals up for adoption. I answered in my usual way, "Adoption, may I help you?" A woman's voice asked, "Yes, I was wondering if you still had a dog named Ricky in adoption?" I said we did. She continued to tell me that her daughter had been down to the shelter several times over the last week and was very interested in

Ricky. I explained that the best thing was to have the daughter come down and fill out an adoption application and we could go from there. She told me her husband was a veterinarian and Ricky would have the finest food and medical attention. This was sounding a little too good to be true.

You have to understand I met many strange people over the years, so I had learned to be cautious. Her daughter was 21 years old, had just moved out on her own and shared an apartment with a childhood girlfriend. Again, I reiterated that it was the daughter I needed to meet with. The woman said she could make it tomorrow. Not getting my hopes up, I said good-bye. Sure enough, in came the daughter the next day. She filled out her application and began by telling me she had seen Ricky on the Sunday, had returned on Tuesday to visit him again, and couldn't stop thinking about him. She had spoken with her dad (the veterinarian) and told him how much she wanted to adopt Ricky. She had worked out how much his food would cost per month, and she could afford it, and her dad had promised to be there for them if needed. All this before we had even started the interview!

She was anxious and nervous, wanting to make a good impression, and I just kept quiet and let her tell me about all the plans she had for Ricky. She continued by telling me that she had overheard some people in the adoption room pointing at Ricky and saying, "He's cute, but he's too old and there's something wrong with him, don't pick him". She said she was so upset by the callousness of some people, she left and cried all the way home.

After completing what was left of the interview, I approved the application for Ricky. We even had the two veterinarians talk to each other regarding any follow-up care. Sometimes I really think that there is a master of fate that comes along when you least expect.

WHY SOME PEOPLE DON'T LIKE DOGS
They follow their owners everywhere.
They stick their cold noses into one's hand at unexpected moments.
They always want to play.
They jump up on their friends and lick them to show their affection.
They bark at people they don't like.

WHY OTHER PEOPLE LIKE DOGS
They follow their owners everywhere.
They stick their cold noses into one's hand at unexpected moments.
They always want to play.
They jump up on their friends and lick them to show their affection.
They bark at people they don't like.

ADOPTING

A

SHELTER

DOG

Off to the Shelter

When you have decided that a shelter is your place of choice for adopting a dog, you will need to understand how your particular shelter operates and what their adoption policies and procedures are. Most shelters will not adopt to anyone under the age of 18.

More than likely, you will be asked to fill out an application so the staff can get an idea of the lifestyle being offered the dog. Please do not take personal offense, or consider these questions an invasion of privacy. Adoption questionnaires are designed to aid staff in the proper and permanent placement of their animals. It is vitally important to correctly match the lifestyle and other variables with the dog chosen.

When you see the rows upon rows of faces looking up at you, try to keep in mind that your first choice may not be best suited for the home you are offering and you may be asked to choose a different dog. Therefore, it is wise to have a pen and paper with you at the time to jot down the cage numbers or names of a few dogs you are interested in. I realize it is extremely emotional and often upsetting to see so many homeless dogs and it can be very overwhelming.

The History
Remember, you are pretty much choosing your dog by physical appearance, age and sex. Any additional information that is on the cage is a bonus. Often staff will include a "history" sheet if available, that is filled out by the previous owner. This may or may not be accurate. Owners want their dogs to be adopted, so they might not be completely truthful. They may "overlook" mentioning certain undesirable traits in hopes of a quick

placement. Unfortunately, this does not help the dog or the new owner and can make unnecessary problems for all involved.

If the dog has come in as a stray, there will be no history sheet. You may find that conscientious staff have made observations during the dog's stay at the shelter and paperwork noting these will usually be attached to the dog's cage. For example, if a dog is keeping the cage clean and is holding elimination for opportunities out of the cage area, you may see a notation that the dog is housebroken.

Do not overlook the dogs that are older. Often these gems are housetrained, not destructive and have an air of dignity and sophistication that goes with maturity. A six- or seven-year-old dog is generally calmer and can adjust to a new life. With the advanced medical technology and specialized veterinarian services provided these days, dogs can live longer and healthier lives. I knew a husband and wife that would only adopt dogs over eight years of age. They usually had two or three dogs at a time and over the course of my career I helped them adopt three dogs in total. They swore that if people knew how wonderful and easy these older dogs were to live with, everyone would be asking for only older dogs.

Adopting A Dog
After you have made a list of possibilities, take the time to solicit the help of shelter staff. They may ask you to fill out your adoption application at this time, so they may get an idea of the home that is being offered. This is where many of the details will be covered. Are there children in the home? Are other pets living in the house? Is the home empty all day or is there someone home during working hours? Are you living in an apartment, condo or private house? Is the yard fenced? What are your prior

experiences with dogs? All this information is important for a successful "match".

To further the process, you may be asked to have all members of the family present at the time of adoption. If there are children involved, the staff will want to be sure that some kind of interaction has taken place prior to finalizing the adoption. This will most likely be in the form of a walk or socializing room outside of the kennel area. If you live with a spouse, brother, roommate, etc., do not be surprised if you are asked to have them accompany you. It is important that the dog chosen is wanted and liked by all who are going to share living space. It would be unfair to the dog if he was returned because a housemate was neither committed to or interested in the particular dog that was chosen.

You would be amazed how many husbands and wives do not even discuss the adoption of a dog. You would think that a decision that requires an investment of 10 to 15 years would be thoroughly discussed before adoption proceeding took place. Yet all too often, a spouse will fill out adoption papers without the other even knowing they are at the shelter. So in the interest of all concerned, make sure the idea of bringing an animal into the home has been properly addressed and agreed to by all those who will be a part of the dog's life. Shelter staff make great efforts on behalf of the animals and take "return" adoptions very seriously. It is very stressful for an animal to be adopted and then brought back because we humans didn't do our homework.

Dogs And Cages
Dogs often react much differently in a smaller confined areas, much like a dog in a parked car, or behind a fenced yard. I was once told by a noted authority on canine behaviour, that in some dogs, aggressive behaviour can increase up to 40% when in a cage behind bars. Some dogs may wiggle and waggle, extending a paw

outward to every passer by, and others will sit with body pressed against the farthest wall, shaking.

All dogs react differently to being in a kennel situation. Some dogs, abandoned by a thoughtless owner, come into the shelter from the streets, where they have gotten used to feeding off garbage, living in filth, cold and other desperate conditions. These dogs would actually refuse to leave the shelter! We would have to literally carry them out for walks and placements. It was a sad sight to see that a shelter environment offered such a great source of security for some of these dear, undeserving strays.

You might be asked to refrain from placing your hands in the cages. This is to help stop the spread of disease and viruses among the dogs. This is extremely important and although it may be hard to resist the friendly gestures made by our homeless friends, you must remember that an outbreak of disease may jeopardize the whole shelter.

If You Already Have A Dog
If you want to add a second dog to a home with an existing dog, many shelters have found that opposite sex matches have been quite successful. I realize this is, however, a general overview, and is certainly not written in stone. If at all possible, ask the staff if it would be acceptable to introduce the two dogs before finalizing adoption papers. A walk around the shelter may provide you with valuable insight as to your choice of "buddies" for your present dog. Usually you will be accompanied by a staff member or experienced volunteer, who will be walking the shelter dog. If your dog does not like the idea and has never been "dog friendly", why push the issue? Be happy with the fact that you have a wonderful companion who is devoted to his/her human pack.

If You Already Have A Cat

Choosing a dog from the shelter that would be compatible with cats can be a little trickier. If the dog has come from a home, most history sheets ask if the dog has been brought up or lived with a cat/s. If the dog is a stray it may be difficult for the staff to assess, due to the fact that dogs and cats are kept in separate areas (for obvious reasons). Most shelter dogs would not have the opportunity to come in contact with cats in this environment. And to waltz a dog through a cat room to see his reaction is highly stressful and most unfair to the cats! So again, I must direct you to the staff to solicit their advise and experience with the dogs that are in their care.

If you are interested in a puppy that is available, there are usually only minimal adjustments to be made, if any. The cat may be a bit frightened at first of the pup and may hiss. Do not force them on each other! I have known puppies that have been scratched in the face because people have tried to push cat and puppy together literally! Let the cat have her space for escape and observation purposes. You may find the cat perched on a high shelf watching this strange new creature that has invaded the house. Leave her be, and in her own time, in her own way she will accept the puppy.

If you have other pets in your home, it would be a good thought to bring the animals' vaccination and health record with you to the shelter. You should also bring current identification with your name and address for verification.

Spaying / Neutering

Spaying is the word used for sterilizing the female dog/cat, and neutering is the term used for male dogs/cats. At some animal shelters the animals will be spayed/neutered before you are permitted to take your new addition home. At other shelters they may ask you whether or not you agree to have the surgery done.

There is absolutely no excuse in this day and age for not having your pet spayed/neutered. Overpopulation is reason enough, but the added health benefits are numerous. Female dogs, after being spayed, will be at less risk of developing mammary cancer, and will not develop any reproductive problems, such as pyometra, ovarian cysts and tumors, and other related, often deadly, problems. All heat cycles will permanently cease. No male dogs will come calling (and they wouldn't if they were neutered), no unsightly discharge, and no need to try and find diapers that fit! The usual time for spaying is six months.

There are so many pluses to neutering the male dog. As far as health goes, the possibility of cancer of the testes is eliminated, and prostate gland problems are greatly reduced. For the male dog the advantages of castration go beyond health into behaviour. Neutered male dogs are less likely to roam. "Marking" is greatly reduced, as is the "mounting" of objects, children, legs, and anything else that strikes a fancy. Fights between male dogs are also greatly reduced. You will have a more manageable, contented "homebody" by neutering the male dog.

I remember an interview I was conducting a number of years ago with a young gentleman who saw no reason for neutering the male dog for which he was applying. I offered valid reasons for the operation, all of which he did not disagree with. He asked me what it entailed and as I explained the simple procedure, he began squirming, crossing his legs, and leaning forward slightly! I assured him that we did not require <u>owners</u> of our dogs to be neutered.

Your Adoption Information
On a final note, when you fill out your adoption application or questionnaire, be certain that you are accurate with the information

you are providing to the shelter staff. Be honest and forthright with all your answers. Don't worry or be embarrassed if you have little or no experience in housebreaking a puppy. It is far easier for staff to educate you, the blank page, than to convince a "know-it-all" to consider other methods.

The only reason I mention this, is because I noticed that some people found the interview process a little threatening, and may have said what they thought I wanted to hear, instead of what they really wanted to say. Sometimes the urge to "fudge" some of the answers to appear more knowledgeable or experienced enters our mind. This is not a wise idea, as information on the application is usually always verified.

Tips For New Pet Owners

The Learning Curve

This section should be titled "We're Home! What Not To Expect" because so many new owners expect the dog to be a mind reader, to understand the English language and to comply with house rules within days after adoption. Learning all these skills takes time. The dog has so many new things to learn and take in. What may have been permitted, or even encouraged, in his previous home, may be strictly forbidden in yours.

New owners often scream and yell at a new dog for a crime he has no idea he committed. This is not very good for the bonding, trusting process. Dogs do not understand what you need or want for some time after you adopt them. They first need to learn how to read you, and then they can do your bidding. You must allow this time on the learning curve.

Some shelter dogs have never seen the inside of a house. They may have been chained to a doghouse all their lives and not possess a sweet clue as to how to behave in a home. I once had a lady call me to tell me she was making dinner and her newly adopted dog had jumped on the counter and had leaned over the frying pan and was in the midst of eating the family supper when the woman turned around. As she screamed in surprise, the dog jumped down. This is only one of many incidents I have heard over the years.

The Language Barrier

If you were in a foreign country, not speaking the native language, trying desperately to ask directions to the nearest restroom, you would probably become frustrated, and even a little frantic. The local people might wonder if you are crazy, as your anxiety increases. Feel the frustration. Understand your anxiety. This is exactly what a new dog feels when you bring him home. You need to keep this in mind as you begin a relationship with your new dog. It illuminates a very important issue.

When I foster, I always find the first two to three days the hardest. Schedule adjustments have to be made, the dog is always full of the ying-yangs from being caged and anxious, and I need to insert the third eye that fits in the back of my head! The situation settles down after a week or two as the routine starts to become familiar, but realistically, transition time is anywhere from four to eight weeks (longer for some dogs and owners). Patience, proper direction, exercise and a good sense of humour are my ingredients for sanity.

The first thing I teach all my foster dogs to do is "sit" using the lure method (see following page). A sitting dog is a dog that is not jumping up, checking out the menu on the counter top, or knocking Aunt Edith down the stairs. There is no need to be pushing the dog's hind end, or even using any physical coercion. I like the "Hands Off" approach to training. It is quite amazing what you can teach with a tiny piece of cheese, a happy voice, and a good attitude.

How To Prevent Destructive Behaviour When Alone
Many owners make the mistake of going to work and letting the new dog have the run of the house. They then return to *a bomb site* and punish the dog. I could write forever just about the stories I have heard on this subject. It has been proven that most destructive behaviour occurs 10-20 minutes after the owner walks out the door and 10-20 minutes before they are due to return (if on a regular schedule). This tells us that it is the act of leaving and the stress of return (anticipating an angry, upset owner who hollers and punishes) that is causing the dog to react.

The Lure Method

1) Take a desired toy or treat (it must be one <u>the dog</u> wants!) Experiment to find several treats your dog enjoys.

2) You can LURE the dog into the sit position by facing your dog and holding the treat just above his/her head. Use the lure, body language and hand gestures (if desired), rather than spoken commands. Be patient if the dog jumps, twirls, tries grabbing at the treat, or tries other positions. Give him credit for being imaginative - and keep trying.

3) Once the desired behaviour is given, **IMMEDIATELY GIVE THE DOG THE TREAT** to make the association. This also tells the dog that his/her fast response time will get a fast response from you!

4) Repeat a few times, then <u>stop</u> until another day, or you will tire out your dog. Keep training sessions short, sweet, fun, and positive.

5) New behaviours can be taught with the same general method. For example, to teach lying down, sit facing your sitting dog, holding the treat above the head. Bring the treat straight down to the floor and then towards you, as if you are tracing an "L". The dog will follow the treat and lie down.

Remember that timing is important, to "lure" the dog into the behaviour you desire. Be careful. If you give the treat <u>as the dog gets up</u> from a sit, you may be rewarding the getting up, not the sitting! Don't get frustrated or yell at the dog. Be quiet, clear and consistent about what you want and it's guaranteed you'll get it.

You must gradually build up the dog's feeling of security about being left alone. This is done in very small increments of time, even seconds. One trainer I know and highly respect starts with stepping out of the door, taking a breath of air, and returning. The initial goal is to be able to take the garbage out without stress to the dog. All dogs are different. This method was designed for extreme cases and if implemented properly works wonders. The message you are trying to get across to the dog is, "Yes, I am leaving, but I always come back". I realize that people of the nineties lead a busy life and that these methods may appear time consuming and slow moving; however, they can easily be incorporated into everyday life.

Do not expect your dog to feel confident about being left alone. The last person the dog trusted and gave his heart to is no longer a part of the dog's life. Sitting in a kennel with little or no social contact appears to make some dogs almost "primed" for attachment. Dogs are social creatures, not programmed to live a life of solitude. We may not even be able to tell whether a dog makes any connection to prior experiences of abandonment, but experience tells us that many of them do. Many shelter dogs, therefore, may follow you like a shadow (even into the washroom) and whine or cry if separated from you, their new friend. Many wiggle out of their skin when the "special person" returns. This may flatter some people because the dog is so devoted and dependent. There is a fine line, however, between loyalty and insecurity.

Start confidence building when you ARE home. Try not to reinforce the "Cling On" syndrome. You can certainly accomplish this in a kind way. For example, praise the dog when he is friendly and confident with other family members and friends who come to visit. Teach the dog "stay" and practice leaving the room, very briefly, and returning. Teach "go to" another family member, that person holding a treat to offer the dog. Then you may move on to frequent visitors. These types of exercises help wean the dog of his over-dependence on one or two people, and broaden his trust in both the owners and other people. Never set up a situation that will scare or "blow" the dog away. This may result in him not trusting YOUR judgment. Go VERY slowly, building on success. Don't force new situations or people on the dog if he's not ready.

Chewing Behaviour
Chewing is a natural behaviour for dogs and they will chew whatever is provided. Rugs, blinds, couches, bedspreads and shoes are not suitable chewies. Therefore, it is up to us to show and teach the dog what is appropriate for munching and giving them the proper items. Kongs, nylabones, gummabones and knotted dental ropes are all good choices.

> Most destructive behaviour occurs 10-20 minutes after the owner walks out the door and 10-20 minutes before the owner is due to return.
>
> This tells us that it is the act of leaving and the stress of return (anticipating an angry, upset owner who hollers and punishes) that is causing the dog to react.

The "Kong" Trick
The best trick I know for combating inappropriate chewing is one I learned at an Ian Dunbar seminar, using a stuffed kong. A kong is a chew toy which resembles a beehive and is made of hard durable rubber, usually black or red in colour, with a hole at the bottom for hiding goodies. Stuff the kong with kibble, cheese, dried liver or peanut butter. This is your "I'm going out, and you are not" saviour. You can stuff the kong the night before and put it away.

The next morning as you are preparing for departure, show the dog this yummy new invention. Let them smell it and pique their interest. Put it away again and continue your morning rituals. Let a few moments pass and get it out again. Show the dog again adding some dramatics, smelling it yourself and pretending you might even pack it in your own lunch box, it looks so good. This may be a bit of a tease, but you really want the dog to say "Please, may I have it, I really NEED that thing!" After you have played out the part and are getting ready to go out, finally give in and let the dog have it. In essence what you want the dog thinking is,

"Man, I wish she would just leave so that I can have that chewie toy and some peace!" All of a sudden your leaving is not so bad; in fact, it's good!

When you return, put the kong away. This act says to your pooch, "Sorry, this extra fun, exciting toy is only for dogs that are alone." Get the connection? Separation made easy!

> **In essence what you want the dog thinking is, "Man, I wish she would just leave so that I can have that chewie toy and some peace!"**
>
> **All of a sudden your leaving is not so bad, in fact, it's good!**

I would still not recommend letting the dog initially have the run of the house. Time frames for training are different for every dog. Either crate train or confine the dog with the use of safety gates. You can safely block off areas that are restricted at this point. Eventually, you can start opening up rooms one at a time as the dog becomes more accustomed to being alone. If you are crating the dog, the kong can be placed in the crate upon your departure. If you prefer to crate train your dog, insure you have introduced the crate in the appropriate fashion. Again, slowly and positively is the way to go. Leaving the crate door open and tossing treats in will hopefully get the dog used to going in and out with ease.

If the dog was crated for very long periods of time in a previous home, or shoved in it for misbehaving, the association to the crate may not be pleasing; in fact, the sight of the crate may cause distress. Try just setting it up and leaving it as a piece of "furniture" for a while. Later you may try leaving treats just outside the open door and eventually throwing them right in. If the dog thinks this crate is a treat dispenser, a more positive view of this "box" may be taken.

I have heard stories of dogs that actually cause physical damage to themselves fighting to get out of a crate. If this is the case, an alternative method should be sought. Often the dogs that do this are so anxiety-ridden they do not even feel the injuries as they are being inflicted. I do not find this the norm, but there have been a few cases and I believe that if the dog is causing bodily harm, it is inhumane to continue crate training.

Exercise Is Crucial!
Adequate exercise is vital for releasing excess energies. Find a fenced-in tennis court that is not occupied and throw a ball or a frisbee, run around and play tag, or just be silly with your dog. Ask a neighbour if your dog can play with their dog in a fenced area, if the two dogs get along. Let them run and chase one another and play as only dogs can. Most dogs enjoy and benefit from the company of their own kind. Join an obedience class that employs kind and humane methods.

Dogs, like people, should exercise the brain more often. Flyball and agility classes are great fun and provide exercise as well as enhancing training skills. I knew a whole team of dogs that played flyball that were all adopted from the shelter. They used to travel around the country for tournaments. If you are a jogger, build the dog up slowly, as you did for yourself, and the two of you can be jogging partners.

Remember, it can be dangerous and cruel to over-exercise a dog - especially an old dog - and be sensitive to temperature and weather conditions. He is, after all, a short-legged creature trying to keep up with a long-legged one. Dogs do not perspire through their skin pores as we do, but rather through their tongues and the pads of their feet. Excessive panting may mean heat stress, a precursor to heat stroke.

A game of hide and seek, even in the house, is exciting, as is hiding some favorite toys and having a scavenger hunt. If you have adopted a dog that is a social butterfly and appears to ENJOY everyone and everything about life in general, inquire about enrolling in a pet therapy class. Nursing homes and retirement facilities are begging for dogs to come and bring smiles and good cheer to the patients. Many therapy dogs have worked miracles in this capacity. Patients who have not spoken a word to anyone in three months will suddenly open up to the visiting dog. There are many good books* (See Appendix) out now on Canine Good Citizen tests and Therapy dogs.

What You Can Do To Entertain Your Pooch

Play hide & seek (in or outdoors)
Have a scavenger toy hunt
Pet therapy
Play soccer
Bake dog biscuits
Fetch the stick or toy
Play frisbee or flyball
Attend agility classes
Find a canine pal to play with
Take a vacation (see guides in Appendix)
Play "catch me if you can" in a yard or fenced area
Join a humane, pet dog training class

The neat thing about exercising/stimulating your dog is that it also creates a sense of camaraderie and kinship, like baking cookies or playing road hockey with your kids. Something magical happens. And don't forget, a good, quiet, relaxing massage or behind the ear scratch goes a long way in the magic department too! I meant for the dog, but you may need one too after all this fresh air and newly acquired exercise program.

A tired dog is a sleeping dog. A sleeping dog is NOT a destructive dog. Some dogs need more exercise than others. Adjust and increase if needed. Hire a mid-day dog walker if you must. It's cheaper than buying new furniture!

Preventing Destructive Behaviour

1) Provide appropriate chewing items. Kongs, nylabones, dental knotted ropes, and gummabones are all good choices. Old shoes, slippers, and socks can not be differentiated from new ones so do not allow dogs to chew on them. Many homemade toys can actually be dangerous as they can be ingested or choked on.

2) Make departures as uneventful as possible.

3) Provide adequate exercise.

4) Do not allow the dog to initially have the run of the house. Use baby gates or a crate if necessary. Four hours (at a time) is the maximum amount of time any dog should be crated. Dogs do not like to be "SHUT" in a closed room.

5) Hire a mid day walker.

6) Never hit or strike your dog. If you come home and something of value has been destroyed, bonk your own head. Be preventative. How did the dog have access to this valuable item? Did you forget to confine or provide acceptable chew toys?

7) Try leaving the radio or television on low.

8) Praise acts of confidence.

House Training

In my fostering experience, I have found that MOST adult shelter dogs are already housebroken. A new environment will cause confusion initially, but once the toileting area has been established, the dogs have caught on very quickly. I find that my own dogs have been able to clearly "teach" or "show" many of the new kids on the block the elimination area. Even if you do not have a resident "expert" on site, this does not mean that housetraining has to be a big ordeal.

Avoid any advice or literature that recommends pushing or shoving the dogs nose into the evacuation.
This is both unkind and unnecessary.
Would you put a dirty diaper or soiled underpants on a toddlers head?

Taking the dog to the desired toilet area and praising for results are the beginnings of proper housebreaking. Go with the dog and stand like a tree. This is not playtime. Save that kind of activity for after the dog has gone to the bathroom. If you have no results after about 10 minutes, take the dog back in the house and either crate him, attach him to your beltloop, or watch him like a hawk! Take the dog out again in 10-15 minutes, repeating the same procedure.

Never hit or strike your dog.
If you come home and something of value has been destroyed, bonk your own head.

Just before a dog needs to relieve himself you may witness a circling motion or sniffing. These are clues to watch for. If you see behaviour like these inside the house, get the attention of the dog sharply with your voice to stop the action from continuing. Whatever word you have used, follow it with the word "OUT" and either scoop the dog, or gently move the dog outside. I say gently because there is no need for dogs being dragged roughly by the scruff of their necks, or hauled out in anger. Remember, having bowel and bladder movements are part of life. All creatures have them! What we need to do is to teach the proper location, not punish the act.

The biggest mistake that people make is they take their dog for a walk in an effort to get the dog to evacuate. I have known some owners who have walked miles for a bowel movement. Unfortunately, what happens is as soon as the dog "performs" the walk is over. It doesn't take the dog long to figure out that going to the toilet ends the walk, and that is the last thing they want to happen, generally speaking, so they hold out as long as possible. What should be happening is that <u>the payoff for a quick elimination</u> in the designated area <u>is the walk</u>. Now you are walking a dog that has an empty bowel and bladder and can actually enjoy your walk, and hey, not too much chance of having to scoop poop in the pitch dark! Carry bags though, just in case.

> **We must learn to speak wisely**
> **and act responsibly**
> **on behalf of those who cannot speak for themselves.**

If an accident indoors is discovered, simply clean it up, and vow to watch the dog more closely. I have heard that a solution of 1/2 water and 1/2 vinegar can be effective, or there are many excellent neutralizers/carpet cleaners that are on the market.

Read Good Training Books
While I have given some advice and guidelines on the most common adjustment problems, many books on the shelves today are full of good information about training and behaviour (**See Appendix). Read as many books as you can BEFORE you bring your new companion home. There are, however, as many different training methods out there as there are authors! If you read something you would clearly not be comfortable implementing, then scrap it. Some methods are cruel and outdated.

With the knowledge we have today about canine development and behaviour there is no reason why owners have to resort to harsh physical methods. What works for you and your dog may not work for the neighbours' dog. Like people, dogs are individuals, each with a different genetic make-up and emotional baggage.

Tips For Housetraining

1) If you can't watch the dog, confine him. Offer outdoor relief as soon as you are finished what you were doing. The dog can be allowed more freedom when he has an empty bowel and bladder.

2) Never, ever, push or shove the dog's face into excrement.

3) Watch for circling and sniffing. This is a clue that the dog needs to go out.

4) Stay with the dog outside and praise for desired results. If there are none, go back in the house, confine for 10 minutes, repeat procedure.

5) If the dog begins eliminating in your presence, stop the action with a sharp voice command, followed by the word/s OUT/OUTSIDE. This is directive as it is specifying a location. As the dog becomes accustomed to the word, you will soon be asking your dog "Do you have to go OUT?"

6) Dogs and especially puppies, tend to eliminate after sleeping, eating and playing.

7) If you want to cue elimination, you can teach words such as "HURRY UP" or "POTTY PLEASE" or whatever words you choose.

Bringing a dog into your life requires adjustments and changes for both parties. Just remember, the reward of sharing your life with a dog is more than worth the time and effort invested.

The Way We Treat Dogs

In 1984, I became obsessed with the behaviour of dogs. My true motivation was seeing the number of abused, stray and misunderstood canines that walked through the shelter doors day in and day out. Normal doggy actions were creating havoc among otherwise well-educated and well-intentioned owners. Barking, chewing, digging, house-soiling, and general rambunctiousness were causing more dogs to become homeless than any other reason. How could this be?

"Major", My First Trainer
I decided to learn all I could to help bridge the gap between human and canine. I read every book I could get my hands on; I attended lectures and seminars and joined a class at an obedience school. I took my father's dog "Major" through the beginner's course. I found everything about obedience training fascinating. During that time Major and I started a new and special relationship, we were communicating in a way I had never experienced before. If people could feel the way I did, I was sure they would never again consider giving up on their dogs. I had been bitten by the obedience bug, yet not for competitive reasons, simply because it helped unclog the communication pipes between dog and owner. I began as an apprentice trainer and continued on to be an instructor.

Bad Advice
I had heard horror stories from other trainers that it was common practice that some so-called "trainers" would "hang" dogs for misbehaving. This means that the poor dog is lifted clear off the ground and suspended in mid air by their leash and collar, leaving the dog choking and breathless. Also, their way to teach down was to have the leash under your foot, command the word "down" and

yank the dog into position. There was a period in the mid-late eighties when every owner in "dogdom" was being taught the importance of being dominant over your "wolf" dog. I once read a list of so- called dominant signs and by the end of the list the dog couldn't even urinate without it being misconstrued as a "challenge" for top dog position.

Owners were being advised to stare, shake, and roll their pets when compliance wasn't obtained. There were more people bitten than there were dogs trained. Then there was and still is, the famous "collar correction". Let's pop, jerk, and snap the dog, sometimes off their feet, into the correct position, all of which, in my opinion is unfair and totally unnecessary. I am not speaking about the occasional collar reminder tug; I am talking about teaching the heel position by constant, inconsistent and untimely leash corrections. A choke collar in the hands of a novice/pet dog handler can be a lethal weapon. There are definitely better, kinder and more humane ways to teach the dog to walk nicely by our side, other than pain avoidance.

Let me put it another way. If you grabbed and pulled your child every time she wandered ahead, two things would happen. First, your child might stay with you to avoid the physical abuse, but wouldn't think much of you. She would fear, not respect you (and secondarily someone would probably call Children's Aid or DYFS). Yet dog owners, through no fault of their own, walk down the street choking, jerking and hydroplaning their dogs, and people walk by and smile considering this to be all in the name of training!

Do Something To Help

I remember last summer, a friend and I were at our nearby park walking and having fun with our dogs. Not too far off was a man with a white Staffordshire terrier mix who was running around. It didn't take us long to figure out the man was trying to get his dog back. He was running after the dog, his arms waving and we could hear him now, and he was mad. His dog came bounding towards him, took one look at his scowling face and turned on a dime running in the opposite direction. After about 10 or so minutes of the histrionics, he grabbed his dog from behind and started beating, screaming, and shaking this bewildered creature. My friend and I looked at each other, we were both stunned. We did intervene, however it was a rude awakening to people's ignorance. I have seen dogs that are getting ready to go to a trial, being slapped for breaking the stay command. Their bodies and self esteem crumble like dry, wilted flowers.

Working in a shelter environment, I have seen the confused, frightened look of dogs on a daily basis. I have witnessed that same look from dogs in obedience schools. Some owners just refuse to accept or believe that their dogs don't understand the commands that are being given, especially at the beginner level. All too often dogs are labeled "aggressive", "dominant" or "stubborn". It's just like that old Gary Larson cartoon. A dog named Fido, for example, initially hears and understands, "Blah, blah, blah, blah, blah, Fido [The dog may say to himself, "Oooh, this guy looks mad, I wonder why?"], blah, blah, blah, blah, blah, bad dog, blah...."

> **We humans are supposed to have the most highly developed brains, yet we continue to use brawn instead...**
>
> **Are we really the brightest animals on the planet?**

If your First Grade child was given a list of spelling words and was clearly having trouble learning them, you would not call the child stubborn. As a parent, you would not become angry, but would find smaller, easier words to start with and build on the child's successes, introducing harder words accordingly.

I had the pleasure of meeting Dr. Roger Mugford when he came to Canada for a lecture and tour, and to visit our shelter. His was a refreshing change from some of the other animal training philosophies and he spent a great deal of time with our staff. He introduced us to his head collar system, The Halti, he explained mimicked the halter worn by a horse. He figured if we could lead a 2,000-lb. horse, it was incomprehensible that we were having such trouble walking our dogs. It all made good sense, but as he warned, many people would think the dogs were wearing muzzles and it would take time for the concept to be accepted. These head collars were widely used in Europe and England and caught on in Canada very quickly. It was just a matter of taking the time to educate the general public. It certainly proved to be a kinder alternative.

In Closing

There have been over 55 foster dogs through our home in the past thirteen years, each one bringing something new and different to our lives.   The stories in this book are just a few of our experiences.

We have fostered immature puppies, dogs with broken bones, and many that had "problems" unique to their personalities and upbringing.   We had one dog that howled like a wolf at the slightest hint of stress, several dogs that were deemed "un-housetrainable", one that used to sleep in my husband's shoe, one that ate my husband's shoe (my fault, of course!), and the list goes on.

Each of our dogs shared a single common thread: the ability to unconditionally accept and give every bit of themselves without question.   No matter our income, our race, creed or colour, marital status, sexual preference, or occupation, dogs take us for who we are, not who others think we should be, or who we want to be. There is no room in their minds for malice, prejudice, or contempt.

I believe dogs are the single most giving, loving, loyal, non-judgmental, and unselfish creatures that share the lives of mankind. If humans were even half as accommodating as dogs, we would become a much better society. Yet we continue to treat them unfairly and unjustly.   We thoughtlessly let them wander; we tie them to doghouses or leave them lonely in our yards, abandon and abuse them. We throw them away when they don't conform to our expectations, just as we would our many disposable products.   We continue to use them for experiments in research laboratories knowing full well the same test has been done a hundred times over. Ignorantly, we continue to allow litter after litter to be born, when there are not nearly enough homes for all.

Humane societies, pounds and shelters strive to promote the welfare of all animals. They cannot (and will never be able to) do it alone. It is up to every one of us to be a part of the solution and not the cause.

I realize that many dogs lead wonderful, rich and fulfilling lives with owners who are responsible beyond the word. Ironically, it will be those same people who are reading this book and I am preaching to the converted.

How You Can Be Part Of The Solution
It may be time to ponder ways in which you can be a part of the solution. If you are a responsible pet owner, see that your local shelter or dog adoption center has some of the ideas contained in this book. Share it with your friends and neighbors. Support humane treatment of animals. And always intervene whenever you are a witness to abuse. You **can** make the world a better place.

Adopting a shelter dog is certainly a major way to help, but try not to let it stop there. We can all do our part to help. A neighbour may need educating on the importance of spaying her cat; or perhaps, a family member may need help in finding a humane way of training their dog, rather than giving up and becoming another statistic. You may spread the word about adopting a shelter animal instead of a pet store purchase. Boy Scouts, Girl Guides, and grade school children all welcome a visitor who will teach them about pets and how to care for them. Everyone has a story or two of their own to share. What better way to set young minds on the road to kindness towards animals? Education is a vital part of bringing an end to the neglect and abuse that face our animal companions every day.

Remember that in order for shelters to continue the life saving work they do, they need continued financial support. Many receive no government funding and rely totally on donations made by the public. If you are not happy or satisfied with your local shelter, then become involved to change policies and procedures that may be outdated, or not in the best interest of the animals.

We must learn to speak wisely and act responsibly on behalf of those who can not speak for themselves.

There are better ways to teach animals other than coercion and compulsion. We humans are supposed to have the most highly developed brain and yet we continue to use brawn. It is far more productive to prevent rather than punish. But today, training dogs has come a long way, with more and more trainers teaching kinder, fairer and more humane methods. Motivating students through games, fun activities, and building on the successes of the dog rather than focusing on what the dog does that we don't like, is the key to a more solid, permanent relationship between owner and dog.

Teaching owners not to take good behaviour for granted is how skilled trainers start to build a strong foundation. If you are searching for a reputable trainer in your area, I would suggest contacting the American Pet Dog Trainers Association if you live in the United States, or if in Canada, The Canadian Association of Professional Pet Dog Trainers.

APPENDIX
Adoption Sources And Resources

Recommended Reading

Doctor Dunbar's Good Little Dog Book
Dr. Ian Dunbar
James and Kenneth Publishers, Berkeley, CA, 1996 (2nd Edition)

Intelligent and Loyal - A Celebration of the Mongrel
Jilly Cooper
Eyre Methuen Ltd., 11 New Fetter Lane, London, England, 1981

Excel-erated Learning
Explaining how dogs learn and how best to teach them
Pamela Reid, Ph.D.
James and Kenneth Publishers, Oakland, CA, 1996

The Animal Shelter
Patricia Curtis
E.P.Dutton, Inc., 2 Park Ave, New York, NY, 1984

Dog Stories
James Herriot
Michael Joseph Ltd., 27 Wrights Lane, Kensington, London, England, 1986

The Culture Clash
Jean Donaldson
James and Kenneth Publishers, Berkeley, CA, 1996

Circles of Compassion:
A Collection of Humane Words and Work
Elaine Sichel (Ed.)
Voice and Vision Publishing, Sebastopol, CA, 1995

Don't Shoot The Dog!
Karen Pryor
A Bantam Book/published by arrangement with Simon and Schuster, New York, NY, 1984

Behaviour Booklets
Ian Dunbar and Gwen Bohnenkamp
James and Kenneth, Oakland CA, 1985

Dog Training the Mugford Way
Roger Mugford
Hutchinson/Stanley Paul, 20 Vauxhall Bridge Rd, London, England, 1992

Dr. Mugford's Casebook
Roger Mugford
Hutchinson/Stanley Paul, London, 1991

Old Dogs, Old Friends
Bonnie Wilcox, DVM and Chris Walkowicz
Howell Book House, New York, NY, 1991

Chicken Soup for the Pet Lover's Soul
Jack Canfield, Mark Victor Hansen, Marty Becker and Carol Kline
Health Communications, Inc., Deerfield Beach, FL, 1998

Training For Dogs In Shelters
Sue Sternberg
Environmentally Cued Training That Transfers

Humane Societies with Good Quarterly Magazines

American Humane Association
63 Inverness Drive East
Englewood, CO 80112
phone 800-227-4645
fax 303-792-5333

Animal Welfare Federation of New Jersey
P.O. Box 467
Madison, NJ 07940
phone 973-783-6812
fax 973-783-5139

ASPCA
424 East 92nd Street
New York, NY 10128
phone 212-876-7700

Animal Sheltering
c/o Companion Animal Section
The Humane Society of the United States
2100 L Street NW
Washington, DC 20037
phone 202-452-1100
fax 301-258-3081

MCE Press
P.O. Box 84 Chester, NJ 07930
Phone **(908) 879-7564 (800) 932-3017**
Email DocMacLean @ aol.com

The Books We Offer:

Nobody's Best Friend by Lorraine Houston
Twelve touching stories of shelter dogs who Lorraine Houston, a world-class dog motivator, has worked with in her lifetime of fostering and caring for dogs. It also includes an Appendix with terrific training techniques (some never seen before!) and practical sections like Adopting A Shelter Dog, The Lure Method, The Language Barrier, Entertainment, The Kong Trick, Preventing Unwanted Behaviour, and Housetraining.
(140pp) Retail Price $12.95 Spiral Trade Paperback (1999) ISBN 09648913-60

Take Your Pet Along-1001 Places To Stay by Heather MacLean Walters
A comprehensive reference to all the pet-friendly hotels, motels, and B&B's across the US and Canada. Includes are costs, amenities, pet-friendly travel tips, all pet travel publications, money-saving coupons, clubs, services, and GREAT web sites!
(320 pp.) Retail Price $14.95 Trade Paperback (1997) ISBN 09648913-28

Take Your Pet Too! Fun Things To Do! by Heather MacLean Walters
A unique reference guide to annual events and exciting places. The only nationwide pet-friendly vacation planner on the market, it includes concerts, galas, cruises, beaches, restaurants, festivals, fairs, dog camps, wine-tastings, museums, and much more! Discount coupons included.
(312 pp.) Retail Price $16.95 Trade Paperback (1997) ISBN 09648913-1X

Nutritional Warfare by Dr. Heather MacLean Walters
A comprehensive and revealing guide that will amaze you with new, vital information critical to good, healthy livingand making informed choices. LEARN THE TRUTH about Irradiation, Pesticides, What To Eat, Antioxidants, Who You Can Trust, Cancer Prevention, Deciphering Food Labels, Viruses In Our Food, Mad Cow Disease, Industry Secrets and Much, Much More!!!
(460+pp) Retail Price $ 17.95 Spiral Trade Paperback (1999) ISBN 09648913-36

The Great Antioxidant Lie by Dr. Heather MacLean Walters
We know that antioxidants prevent cancer, and yet we keep hearing new studies that say that a certain ANTIOXIDANT CAUSES CANCER? How can that be? The Great Antioxidant Lie has a common sense hypothesis that could save your life and the lives of your family and friends. Read about topics like: Is Your Cereal KILLING You? Why COFFEE may be your best vitamin! Are there antioxidants in CIGARETTES? Take the new anticancer pill (angiostatin) for almost no cost, with no prescription!!!
(185pp) Retail Price $15.95 Spiral Trade Paperback (1999) ISBN 09648913-44

The Philology Of Taste by Professor Harry Randall
Subtitled "The Wayward Language Of Food", this wonderful coffeetable book explores the relationship of words about food and why we use them. It shows us how the words we use to describe our favorite meals reveal our most personal desires. From *scullery* and the story of *stone soup* to the derivation of *al forno* and *frangipani*, the Professor knows all and tells all.
(135pp) Retail Price $24.95 Hardcover / Illus. (1995)

MCE Order Form

Name: _____

Address: _____

City/State/Zip: _____

Phone Number _____

Payment: ☐ Check ☐ Money Order ☐ American Express:

Card Number: _____

Expiration Date: _____

Take Your Pet Along-1001 Places To Stay	**$14.95**
Hotels, motels, and pet-friendly B&Bs 320pp (1997)	
Take Your Pet Too! Fun Things to Do!	**$16.95**
Vacation planner w/ fairs, festivals, cruises, etc. 312pp (1997)	
Nobody's Best Friend	**$12.95**
12 touching tales of shelter dogs who were saved 140pp (1999)	
Nutritional Warfare	**$17.95**
A comprehensive, revealing guide to preventive eating 460+pp (1999)	
The Great Antioxidant Lie	**$15.95**
The real truth about antioxidants -both bad and good 185pp (1999)	
The Philology Of Taste	**$24.95**
An amusing look a the wayward language of food 135pp (1995)	

Receive a 10% discount on two or three books
Receive a 20% discount on any four or more
[Call 800-932-3017 for further bulk discounts]

Total Order	**$.**
Shipping & Handling	
($3.00 each book-to $9.00 total for any order/any # books)	**$.**
Tax (6% if you are a NJ resident)	**$.**
TOTAL	**$.**

It's Summer! You're planning a great vacation...but will you leave someone *sad and hairy* behind?

Don't break the dog's heart-**TAKE YOUR PET ALONG!**

Take Your Pet Along-1001 Places To Stay
Heather MacLean Walters for MCE Press
A comprehensive reference to all the pet-friendly hotels, motels, and B&B's across the US and Canada. Includes are costs, amenities, pet-friendly travel tips, all pet travel publications, money-saving coupons, clubs, services, and GREAT web sites!
(320 pp.) Retail Price $14.95 (1997) ISBN 09648913-28

Take Your Pet Too! Fun Things To Do!
by Heather MacLean Walters for MCE Press
A unique reference guide to annual events and exciting places. The only nationwide pet-friendly vacation planner on the market, it includes concerts, galas, cruises, beaches, restaurants, festivals, fairs, dog camps, wine-tastings, museums, and much more! Featured in **U.S. News & World Report**, **Prevention, New Woman**, and many others. Discount coupons included.
(312 pp.) Retail Price $16.95 (1997) ISBN 09648913-1X

About The Author

Lorraine H. Houston has devoted the past 16 years to the welfare of abandoned and mistreated dogs. She began her career with the Toronto Humane Society, where she served as Supervisor of the Adoption Department for nine years. She was instrumental in the development of the shelter's foster program, which has saved the lives of thousands of dogs, personally fostering over 50 animals. Featured in numerous television specials for THS, she has been seen by millions of viewers across Canada. She also founded her own dog training school and adoption service, Canine Connections.

Ms. Houston is a past president of the Scarborough branch of the Ontario SPCA, a member of the Canadian Association of Professional Pet Dog Trainers, and a Certified Animal Control Officer. Currently she is the shelter manager for Noah's Ark Animal Welfare Association, a non-profit shelter in the New York metropolitan area. She resides in Morristown, New Jersey with her husband, two sons, four dogs and one cat.